When Freedom Is Lost
The Dark Side of the Relationship between Government and the Fort Hope Band

The devastating impact of the policies and programs of the federal government on the Indian people of Canada is illustrated forcefully in this important and revealing study of the Fort Hope band.

Over a period of seven years, the authors looked at the communities of Webequie, Summer Beaver, Lansdowne House, and Fort Hope in the far reaches of northwestern Ontario, seeking answers to such questions as: How do a people become wards of the state? How does a government work against its stated objectives? How do ghettos appear in the middle of a pristine wilderness?

They found that, starting in the early '60s, as government involvement in band life increased, dependency on government also increased – to the point where today government programs provide 90 per cent of the band members' income.

Government's failings were many. Government projects hired too many workers and encouraged inefficiency and waste. High school students were forced to abandon their parents and placed in a no-man's world. The community was allowed to drift into anarchy where drunkenness and violence became a way of life.

The authors also found that government bureaucrats held virtually all control over the band yet were never accountable to it; that government agencies operated without clear or workable objectives and failed to monitor or assess projects once they were in place. They discovered at the same time that civil servants believed that band members were responsible for all business failure and all social breakdown.

Now dependent on programs which can be curtailed at the government's will, the band is in an extremely vulnerable position. The authors suggest that this is also true of other bands across the country, and offer suggestions for constructive change.

PAUL DRIBEN is chairman of the Department of Anthropology and director of Native Studies at Lakehead University.

ROBERT S. TRUDEAU is regional superintendent for the Department of Economic Development and Tourism, Government of the Northwest Territories.

PAUL DRIBEN
ROBERT S. TRUDEAU

When Freedom Is Lost:
The Dark Side of
the Relationship between
Government and
the Fort Hope Band

UNIVERSITY OF TORONTO PRESS
Toronto Buffalo London

© University of Toronto Press 1983
Toronto Buffalo London
Printed in Canada

ISBN 0-8020-2506-4 cloth
ISBN 0-8020-6526-0 paper

Canadian Cataloguing in Publication Data

Driben, Paul, 1946–
When freedom is lost

Bibliography: p
Includes index
ISBN 0-8020-2506-4 (bound) — ISBN 0-8020-6526-0 (pbk)

1. Ojibwa Indians.   2. Indians of North America – Ontario – Fort Hope (Indian reserve) – Government relations.   3. Indians of North America – Ontario – Fort Hope (Indian reserve) – Economic conditions.   4. Indians, Treatment of – Ontario – Fort Hope (Indian reserve).   I. Trudeau, Robert S. (Robert Sanderson), 1945–   II. Title.

E92.D74   323.1'197'0713112   C83-098574-3

42,150

Contents

Photographs

Preface

In 1964 the Indian Affairs Branch of the Department of Citizenship and Immigration asked the University of British Columbia to prepare a report on the economic, political, and educational needs of Canada's Indians. Professor Harry Hawthorn was in charge of the project, which investigated the life-style of approximately 35,000 of the 200,000 Indians in the country, and in 1967 the findings were published in a landmark document titled *A Survey of the Contemporary Indians of Canada*.

The Hawthorn Report presented a dismal picture of Indian life, especially of their economy. To show just how far the Indians had fallen behind, it pointed out that while the average Canadian earned approximately $1,400 per year, Indians earned only about $300 per year. The report also confirmed that an unusually large proportion of Canada's Indians depended on welfare and social assistance for their livelihood. It said that on certain reserves more than half the people were on welfare at any given time and that the per capita cost of social assistance for Indians was twenty-two times the national average.[2]

These findings were a serious blow to the federal government. Its policies and programs for Indians had failed. A new strategy would have to be developed, and to this end Hawthorn and his associates proposed ninety-one recommendations, most of which called on the government to increase its expenditures on the 2,241 reserves in the country. The thirteenth recommendation is one of the best examples of the report's emphasis on increased public funding to solve the Indians' problems: 'An adequate program for economic development of Indians will require public expenditures on their behalf in the hundreds of millions of dollars per annum over the foreseeable future. This will entail a much larger budget and staff for the Indian Affairs Branch, as well as more assistance from other government agencies at all levels.'[3]

The federal response to the Hawthorn Report was unusually quick. In 1969, Jean Chrétien, minister of Indian Affairs and Northern Development, came forward with a White Paper on Indian policy.[4] It was the newly elected Trudeau government's reply to the issues Hawthorn had raised, and it promised that Indians no longer would be treated as second-class citizens. They would be given an opportunity to participate in Canadian society on an equal footing with the rest of the population, and in the economic sphere this meant exactly what Hawthorn had proposed in his thirteenth recommendation, namely, more money for economic development and new programs to bring Indian people into the mainstream of the national economy.

The White Paper marked the beginning of a new economic era for Indians. Millions of dollars were allocated to establish Indian businesses; job-training programs were conducted on isolated reserves, and make-work and community-development programs were introduced where none had existed before. But even though more than a decade has passed since these measures were taken, there has been absolutely no improvement in the Indians' situation. In 1978, a federally appointed task force concluded that, 'despite substantial expenditures on programs to increase Native employment, unemployment remains at an unacceptably high level.'[5] Recent studies bear this out. Current estimates place the ratio of employed to dependent people in Indian communities at 1:10, compared to 1:2 in the country at large.[6]

To make matters worse, Indian people have become completely frustrated by White Paper programs. Harold Cardinal, one of the leading Indian spokesmen in the country, summed things up:

So it goes – half truths, outright lies, plain bullshit. The facts are we don't get the jobs, we don't get the training, we don't get the resources to help us help ourselves. It's a damned lie to say that we are a pluralistic society that tries to give opportunities to all the people to develop on their own terms so that we can all have a beautiful Canada to live in. That's not what is happening where it counts most.

That's not what is happening if you are an Indian and have no political clout. It's bullshit. The situation in which our people find themselves is just too damned bad to put up with bullshit any longer.[7]

This book is about the political and economic relationships that developed between the Ojibwa Indians in the Fort Hope Band[8] and their government agents before and after the White Paper was introduced. It describes a system that keeps almost 1,500 Indian people dependent and subservient to government, angers Indian leaders such as Cardinal, and makes task forces complain about unacceptable results. It is also a condemnation of the White Paper and the programs it spawned.

Many of the facts and arguments in the chapters that follow were brought to the attention of both the federal and Ontario governments in 1976. We did this to fulfil an obligation we had agreed to one year earlier when we were hired by the Department of Manpower and Immigration[9] to conduct a socio-economic study of the Fort Hope Band under the auspices of LEAP, Manpower's Local Employment Assistance Program.

The research was undertaken to discover a way to help lead the band out of the morass of government dependency into which it had fallen. More specifically, we were to find out the extent to which band members were dependent on government funds, the causes of their dependency, and how the situation could be improved through economic development. In line with these objectives we produced a report that documented how the White Paper had encouraged band members to become dependent on government, how their businesses had failed, how one of the band communities might soon be abandoned, and how government agencies were responsible for this state of affairs by virtue of the misguided initiatives they had undertaken to help the band. The report also indicated how some of these problems could be solved.

Since then the government not only has failed to take remedial action; it has compounded the problem. In the meantime we have been able to gather additional information and reflect on our original ideas. This book is the result of that process.

Acknowledgments

The research on which this book is based was carried out with the help of many people. We would like to take this opportunity to thank them.

From the Department of Indian Affairs and Northern Development: Mansel Barstow, Jack Carrol, Ted Gardner, Barry Gibb, Bob Readman, and Violet Summers.

From the Department of Manpower and Immigration: John Del Ben, George Macdonald, and George Richmond.

From the Fort Hope Band: Elizabeth Atlookan, Charlie Boyce, Barbara Kitchejohn, Fanny Kitchejohn, Eli Moonias, Marceline Moonias, Peter Moonias, Corne Nate, Daisy Neshnapaise, Ellen Neshnapaise, Bert Sanders, Matthias Saganaqueb, Solomon Saganaqueb, Bill Shawinimash, Roy Wabase, Daisy Waswa, Louis Waswa, Andy Yesno, and Christine Yesno.

From Lakehead University: Ken Dawson and El Molto.

From the Ministry of Culture and Recreation: John Cosgrove.

From the Ministry of Natural Resources: John Cleavely, John Gow, and Doug Sayer.

From the Sioux Lookout Zone Hospital: Gary Goldthorpe.

From the University of Toronto: Larry Sawchuk.

From the University of Toronto Press: R.I.K. Davidson.

We would also like to thank Mansel Barstow, Don Worrall, and DIAND for the use of their photographs, and Iain Hastie, who prepared our figures and maps.

Nor could this book have been written without the help and encouragement of Carol Driben.

Although we take full responsibility for any errors, without these people this book would have been impossible.

This book has been published with the help of a grant from the Social

Science Federation of Canada, using funds provided by the Social Sciences and Humanities Research Council of Canada.

P.D.
R.S.T.

WHEN FREEDOM IS LOST

1

Introduction

Northern Ontario, above the CNR line, is an immense tract of land more than half the size of the province. It is a remote, isolated wilderness region, and except for about thirty scattered Indian communities and a handful of small towns, there are no other settlements. It is within the central and northern part of this territory, impenetrable except by canoe and plane, that the Ojibwa Indians who belong to the Fort Hope Band live.

The band is one of 115 in Ontario[1] defined by the Indian Act as groups whose land and money are held in perpetual trust by the federal government. Roughly two thousand people belong to the Fort Hope Band, and most of them live in four small villages between the Albany River and the Winisk.[2] The names of the villages are Fort Hope, Webequie, Lansdowne House, and Summer Beaver. Among them, only Fort Hope is located inside the band's 160-square-kilometre reserve.[3] The others are situated on land owned by the province, far removed from the reserve and to the north-west – Lansdowne House 80 kilometres away, Summer Beaver 160, and Webequie more than 240 (see Map 1).[4]

The Department of Indian Affairs and Northern Development (DIAND) operates elementary schools in the communities in accord with Treaty No 9, which the band's ancestors signed in 1905. Teachers are usually non-Indians from large urban centres in southern Ontario, and to introduce them to the places in which they will be working, DIAND's district office in Geraldton provides a mimeographed pamphlet that describes the villages in picturesque terms.[5] Hunting, fishing, snow-shoeing, canoeing, hiking, snowmobiling, cross-country skiing, and photography are all mentioned as possible pastimes. It could be added that the landscape is beautiful; wildlife is plentiful; transportation is available on DC 3s or small

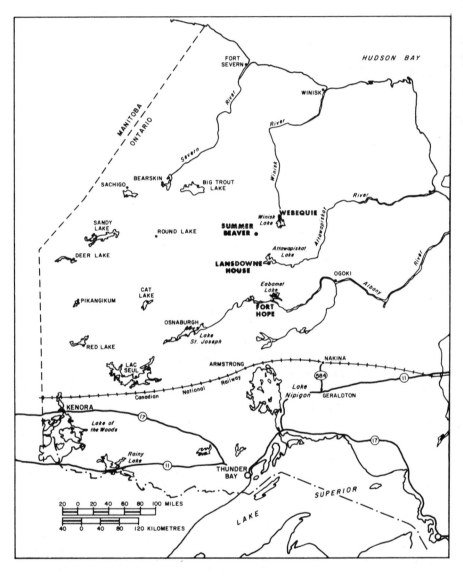

MAP 1

The Fort Hope Indian Reserve, Lansdowne House, Summer Beaver, Webequie, and surrounding territory

charter aircraft; shopping is done at co-operatives, the Bay, or by mail-order from Sears; and long-distance telephone calls can be made via satellite relay. One is almost left with the impression that the communities are northern resorts with all the comforts of home, yet still almost 250 kilometres north of the nearest highway by plane. However, that impression is misleading. The band communities are far more complex and differ from each other in significant ways.

Fort Hope

The village of Fort Hope is located on the north shore of Eabamet Lake in the south-western corner of the band's reserve. Before the reserve was created, Eabamet Lake was the site of an important Hudson's Bay Company post where the band's ancestors traded their furs for European goods and supplies. When the heyday of the fur trade had passed, the people began to settle near the post, and by the midpoint of this century it was surrounded by a tiny collection of makeshift log houses and shacks. The original townsite, which was located on the south shore of Eabamet Lake, was moved to its present location in 1962, and following the move the community took on an entirely different appearance.

The new townsite was planned by DIAND's predecessor, the Indian Affairs Branch of the Department of Citizenship and Immigration. To minimize the cost of providing the residents with water, electricity, and other services that the Branch promised to install, the houses and buildings were erected in tight parallel rows separated by wide dirt roads. There are no cars and only two half-ton trucks in the community, so the roads are used mainly as sidewalks or for motorcycles and snowmachines. In spite of this, one is left with the impression of order and organization usually associated with the south, save for the fact that the village is surrounded entirely by wilderness. Fort Hope is also the band's largest community and its administrative centre. Nearly 660 people live there,[6] including the chief and council and a handful of non-Indians who work as teachers, nurses, or for the Bay. Ever since the treaty was signed, Fort Hope has also been the place where most government officials conduct their business with the band, and today this means that it is an extremely busy place, with aircraft in and out almost every day.

Webequie

Webequie has a different impact on visitors, although it too grew around an old Hudson's Bay Company post. It is located on an island in Winisk

River Provincial Park, and with a population of 400 it is the second largest community in the band.[7] In appearance Webequie represents a good mix of the old and the new. On the west side of the island there is a modern group of standard, wood-frame government houses, and balanced against them on the east are a number of older dwellings, many still of log construction. But the most striking feature of Webequie is found on a high rocky hill in the centre of the community, where a white picket fence encircles a small enclave of old cabins and a weather-beaten church. The fence, residents says, is to keep out intruders and was built to show that the houses and church are on protected, sanctified ground. On the outskirts of the village the landscape is dotted with a myriad of lakes, so many that government officials wisely advise inexperienced tourists to hire a guide to avoid getting lost.

Summer Beaver

Summer Beaver is the newest band community. It was established in 1976 by a breakaway group from Lansdowne House and is by far the most idyllic of the four villages. It has a small population, only 137 people,[8] and is situated on the edge of a tiny, peaceful lake in a thick forest of tall evergreen trees. All of the houses in Summer Beaver are spaced well apart and built entirely from logs, as are the government school and the nursing station. In fact, nothing appears to be out of place in Summer Beaver. One question often asked is why the other band communities are not equally attractive. The answer is that Summer Beaver was planned and built by the people who live there, initially with no government assistance because senior officials refused to lend their support.

Lansdowne House

Finally, there is Lansdowne House, the community that gave rise to Summer Beaver, and in many ways no stronger contrast could exist. About 235 people live in Lansdowne,[9] but in spite of its size there is no planned organization as in Fort Hope and Summer Beaver and far less than in Webequie. Instead, the village consists of a jumble of houses, half of them empty, and a ragtag collection of buildings unevenly spread out over two small islands joined by a narrow wooden bridge. The characters of the islands are distinct, almost opposite. The smaller island,

'Couture Island,' named after an early Catholic missionary, is solitary in appearance and contains a church, a rectory, a co-op store, a small sawmill, and a few log cabins. The larger island, the 'Mainland,' with graffiti scrawled on buildings, scattered oil drums, and seemingly endless debris, looks altogether squalid and slum-like. Lansdowne House is also generally considered to be the most troubled of the band's villages and has the unenviable reputation of being one of the most violent Indian communities in northern Ontario. Public drunkenness, fist-fights, and vandalism are all commonplace and part of village life. Seeing young children lying on the ground in an unconscious stupor from sniffing gasoline is also not uncommon.

Our first night

By coincidence, Lansdowne House was the first band community we visited. Almost everyone we talked to before we arrived there in July 1975 had warned us about Lansdowne, but we were still ill-prepared for what we saw.

When our plane landed in the late afternoon, there was trouble in the village: people were drinking, and the atmosphere was tense. That night a gang of young men beat up a young Indian woman, spreading fear through the entire community. A white teacher who had been living in Lansdowne House for more than a year told us about his encounter with the gang:

I went over to the nursing station around six in the evening, stayed for supper, and after a couple of hours decided it was time to go home. I looked outside and it was quiet, so I started to get ready to leave. Even when one of the nurses told me to be careful, I still didn't think much about it. So I started on my way back along the boardwalk.

It was clear out, and I could see almost everything. Then, in the distance, I saw the drunks, twelve, maybe more, moving around and yelling at the top of their lungs. I thought some of them had knives, but they were still far away and it was hard for me to tell.

When I saw them out there weaving around I knew they could see me, and I started to think, 'They're going to come after me and beat the shit out of me!'

Now I didn't want to go back to the nursing station because I didn't want to get the reputation of being a 'chickenshit' with the nurses. And besides,

I thought the drunks would just hide and wait until I came out again. So there was nothing left to do but leave the boardwalk and go around over the muskeg. I figured I could outmanoeuvre them by going around in a wide sweep.

The problem with that was that pretty soon I was so far out I couldn't see anything. So I hid there in the muskeg, away from the village, hearing the drunks move and yell not too far off, imagining all sorts of crazy things until finally it started to quiet down and I made my escape to my house.

The next day we saw for ourselves what the community was like. Three young men, reputedly the most violent, were tied to trees. That had been done to sober them up by a two-man detachment from the Ontario Provincial Police that had flown in that morning.[10] A small crowd of older men and a few women and children stood to one side, seemingly disinterested in the spectacle they were watching and yet talking about it quietly and seriously among themselves.

As it turned out, they were frightened and angry, and complained bitterly to us that the police were never around until it was too late; we found out later that sometimes the drinking and violence got so bad that people simply headed for the bush until the police arrived. When we asked the bystanders why there was so much trouble in Lansdowne, one old woman said, 'It's him that's responsible,' and she pointed to one of the young men in ropes. We were told that he was the ringleader, the one who had arranged to bring in the liquor by chartered plane and the one who had led his friends on the rampage the night before.

Front-page news

As an epitaph to the scene in front of us, a visiting DIAND official took us aside and said, 'This place is only going to get worse.' As it turned out, he was right. Two years later, in 1977, violence in Lansdowne House reached epidemic proportions. Three white teachers were attacked by a group of young men, and the community's problems were catapulted on to the front page of a daily newspaper in the south. The headline read 'VIOLENCE FORCES SCHOOL TO CLOSE,' and the accompanying story went on to explain that DIAND was not going to reopen the school in Lansdowne until vandalism and alcohol abuse were curtailed – a process that was 'up to the community itself.' The article also pointed out that it was mainly those in their early twenties who were responsible for the trouble.[11]

After some hard bargaining and a lull in the trouble the school was reopened, but the peace was not to last. A year later, in 1978, Lansdowne House was again brought to the attention of the reading public, only this time the audience was international. In an article that appeared in *National Geographic*, the community was described as follows:

Can the plight of Ontario's Indians really be that grim? ...

The village of Lansdowne House near Fort Hope is a place where most hope has faded away.

Few earned dollars come into the community – though a handful of Indians operate a commercial fishing enterprise. For the most part, though, Lansdowne House lives on welfare. And in government-built houses, without running water, without sewers, many of them uncared for wrecks. Much of life at Lansdowne is sullen; some of it is drunken. [12]

But by the time this story appeared, violence, vandalism, and alcohol abuse were not the only problems in Lansdowne. Half the people already had moved to Summer Beaver; others were preparing to leave, and the community's economy was in ruins.

The root of the problem

Although we never saw the same kind of social disintegration in the other band communities that we witnessed in Lansdowne, we did find out that they all had experienced far more than their fair share of change and were suffering from a deep economic malaise. In the months we spent in the villages talking to people and going through records, we learned that up until the early 1960s, band members were still living off the land much as their ancestors had done, hunting, fishing, and trapping. But beginning in the 1960s their world began to change. Government schools were built in what are now their villages, and the people were encouraged to settle and adapt to village life. But living in villages made them less effective at living off the land, so the people turned to welfare and social assistance to support themselves, which made them increasingly dependent on government. Then, in 1969, the government's White Paper was ostensibly brought forward to help them and other chronically unemployed Indian people escape from the dependency into which they had fallen. Unfortunately, the new policy only made them more dependent. By 1975, government was providing the band with almost 90 per cent of its 1.4 million dollars in disposable income, more than half that amount coming from White Paper programs alone. Today, there is little doubt that if these make-work, job-training, community-development, and job-creation programs are removed, the band's economy will collapse.

However, the belief that this was done deliberately, through some secret plan to keep Indian people subservient to government, is not one that we share. To argue that keeping Indian people in need of government is somehow in the government's best interests is to miss the point that government resources are drained when this occurs and that Indian people are thereby prevented from contributing to the national economy. It simply does not make good economic sense to keep Indian people dependent on government.

Rather, the band's current economic dilemma is rooted in the zeal that characterized the way government agencies promoted their White Paper initiatives in the band and in the paternalistic methods they used to deliver their programs. Instead of beginning with a clear set of workable objectives that were consistent with what the people wanted, government agencies such as DIAND and Manpower almost always worked at cross-purposes, failed to monitor and assess their programs, and, worst of all, never really consulted with the people they were supposed to be serving. The outcome was that band members were rewarded for becoming dependent, stymied in their attempts to become independent, and left in a position where vulnerability to government cut-backs is now the one overriding feature of their lives. Nor do we believe that the Fort Hope experience is unique, only an unfortunate example of what has happened and is continuing to happen to Indian people living in remote, economically depressed areas of the country.

2

Before government

It is difficult, perhaps even in some ways impossible, to appreciate the drastic changes that the people in the Fort Hope Band have gone through during the past few years without understanding something of their history. For instance, it was not until the beginning of this century that the government made a treaty with the Fort Hope people, and it was not until the 1960s that the government became heavily involved in their affairs. The band's ancestors did not even begin to interact with Europeans in a significant way until the middle of the eighteenth century, when the Ojibwa became directly involved in the fur trade. Before then, during pre-contact times, they lived their lives in a completely different way. They called it 'a-da-wah-gee-gay-win,' which means going after game. It is with this period that we begin the band's story, a time when their ancestors were a fully independent people and one that stands out in stark contrast to the situation that exists today.

Going after game: prehistory to 1750

The origin of the Fort Hope Band can be traced to the aboriginal Ojibwa,[1] who occupied a rich belt of land along the north shore of Lake Superior, stretching from the shoreline north to the height of land (see Map 2). Based on the reports of missionaries and explorers who lived among the Ojibwa, anthropologists believe that the aboriginal population contained about 4,500 people, distributed among twenty or so lakeside and river-mouth camps.[2] It has also been estimated that the camps usually contained anywhere from 100 to 300 people,[3] although at the mouth of the St Mary's River, where the city of Sault Ste Marie now stands, the population may have been as high as 1,000.[4]

The annual round

During pre-contact times the camps were well-integrated communities – places where people could learn, play, marry, make friends, participate in sacred rituals, and become involved in all the other social activities that make community life enjoyable. There was also an abundance of food. The Ojibwa were expert fishermen, and during the summer they captured large amounts of whitefish, lake trout, pickerel, pike, and sturgeon. They also relied on hunting and gathering to support themselves. Small game animals, birds, wild rice, and berries were all popular summer foods. But as winter approached the environment changed, and towards the latter part of autumn, as was their custom, the Ojibwa divided themselves into small family groups, broke camp, and headed north in search of large game animals such as moose, woodland caribou, and bear.

During winter, hunting was the principal occupation of the Ojibwa. Since the animals they hunted provided them with substantial amounts of protein and fat, the people were rarely undernourished,[5] and if game was not available in one location, they could always move to another since the land was regarded as something that belonged to the entire tribe.[6] In this way each small band of hunters was almost always certain that it could get enough food to survive. When winter came to an end, the Ojibwa returned to their summer camps, where they remained until it was time to move north and begin hunting again.

Aboriginal society

The climate and character of the northern environment also helped shape the structure of early Ojibwa society. Since fish and game were captured in different areas at different times of the year, the people were never able to establish large, permanent settlements with a central government as did agricultural tribes such as the Huron. They were simply never in one place long enough to form communities of that sort. Nevertheless, they did develop a social organization that was eminently suited to their own objectives.

On the tribal level the Ojibwa were joined together through patrilineal clans.[7] Each clan was named after an important mythical ancestor who helped create the earth.[8] A person became a member of a clan at birth and regarded his clanmates as lifelong blood relations whom he was obligated to help and who were obligated to help him in return. Since members of the same clan were regarded as blood relations, marriages were arranged between members of different clans – otherwise the marriages would have been considered incestuous – and this forged links between the clans that ultimately united the Ojibwa into a single body or tribe.

Clans are not always easy to maintain. Since camps composed of several clans or even clan segments can contain hundreds of people, food is of paramount importance. In summer this was not a significant problem because there were enough fish in the lakes and rivers where the Ojibwa camped to support large groups. But in winter it was virtually impossible for clans to remain together because hunting for animals such as moose and woodland caribou requires rapid movement across vast tracks of land, and this is something that large groups of people simply cannot do in the dense cover of the northern forest. Under these circumstances the Ojibwa were obliged to subdivide their summer communities into much smaller social units for the winter.

From October until the ice broke apart in April, the mainstay of Ojibwa society was the hunting party. Hunting parties generally contained around fifty people who were related through patrilineal descent. Often the main parties were composed of even smaller secondary groups, which would hunt as independent or semi-independent units although they would still usually share the same base camp.[9] Then, at the beginning of spring, the people would begin to reunite until the process was completed in their summer camps.

It is also worthwhile pointing out that during pre-contact times the Ojibwa did not rely on trapping to any great extent. Although animals such as beaver and rabbit were used to make clothing and blankets, the aboriginal demand for furs was relatively low.[10] Beaver, for instance, were hunted more for their meat than for their pelts. Even after the Ojibwa did begin to exchange furs for European goods at the end of the seventeenth century, hunting, fishing, and gathering continued to be their main occupations for another fifty years.

The fur trade: 1750 to 1905

When the ancestors of the Fort Hope Band began to participate in the fur trade, they were no doubt unaware of the impact it would have on their social and economic lives. They became involved in the trade almost by accident. In fact, although French and British traders were buying furs

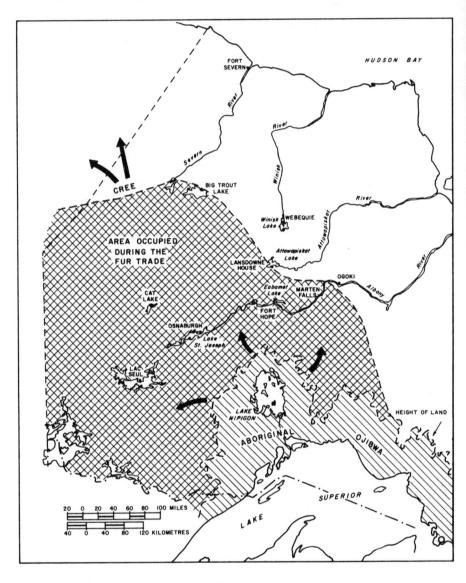

MAP 2

The expansion of Ojibwa territory during the fur trade

SEE Bishop *The Northern Ojibwa and the Fur Trade* 332.

in the Ottawa Valley and on the south shore of Hudson Bay as early as the late 1600s, the Ojibwa were involved only incidentally. At that time they traded mainly with other Indians.

The situation changed when the Cree, who occupied the territory north of the Ojibwa, began to move west in conjunction with the expansion of the Hudson's Bay Company during the seventeenth and eighteenth centuries.[11] The Cree were the main provisioners and trading partners of the Bay, and their move to the west produced a vacuum in what is now northern Ontario. French competitors were quick to take advantage, and from 1713 until French rule ended in Canada in 1759, they built a number of posts in the vacant area.[12] The French were also looking for a tribe that would supply their posts with furs, so they encouraged the Ojibwa to enter the trade by offering them goods such as guns, powder, hatchets, knives, kettles, and other items the people could not manufacture from the land.[13] The new technology became increasingly important to the Ojibwa, and by the middle of the eighteenth century many of them had abandoned their southern territory in favour of a permanent home in the north (see Map 2).[14]

Trapping units

The Ojibwa adjusted to the move north and the new emphasis on trapping and trading by revamping their social organization. Since clans and even hunting parties were too large to work effectively in the boreal forest, they were replaced by the trapping unit, which usually contained only about twenty people who were members of the same patrilineal extended family, that is, 'a group of patrilineally related males, unmarried females, and the wives of the males under the leadership of the eldest male.'[15] These groups were extremely effective for two reasons. First, because they were small, they placed little pressure on the animal populations they hunted and trapped, and this guaranteed their members a steady supply of meat and furs. Second, because they were mobile, the Ojibwa were able to go from one trading post to another, and this protected their bargaining power in the trade.[16] The mobility of trapping units also made it possible for the people to maintain their social contacts, especially in spring and summer, when two or more groups would travel together and trade their furs at the same post.

The success of trapping units, however, was short-lived. During the first three decades of the nineteenth century two events occurred that changed the way the Ojibwa lived in a dramatic way. One was the amalgamation of the Hudson's Bay Company and its main rival, the North West Company, in 1821. This restricted competition between fur buyers, and the Ojibwa lost the economic advantage they had obtained by travelling from one trading post to another. Around the same time most of the large game animals in north-western Ontario disappeared,[17] and, fearing they would starve, the people became reluctant to travel too far away from the Hudson's Bay Company posts where they bought their supplies.

Staying by the posts

By 1830 the food shortage had become critical, and many Ojibwa were forced to depend on fish and rabbits to feed themselves.[18] Since they were living by the posts, they were also unable to trap fur-bearing animals in outlying regions, and this placed them under tremendous economic strain.[19] Unfortunately, these harsh conditions persisted until the turn of this century. By then large game animals had returned, but in the interim the European demand for furs had diminished. The heyday of the fur trade had passed, and the Ojibwa were unable to recapture the power they had once possessed in the trade. Instead, small bands of Ojibwa continued to rely on Hudson's Bay Company posts such as the one at Fort Hope, which was an old North West Company post refurbished by the Bay in 1890, and its outposts at Webequie and Lansdowne House.[20] Although they were still able to trade their furs at these posts, hunting, fishing, and gathering had once again become just as important to the people as trapping.

The return to these older economic endeavours had a significant impact on the social organization of the Ojibwa. By the beginning of this century trapping units had become less formal, and clan relationships had lost most of their traditional importance. Alanson Skinner, an anthropologist who visited Fort Hope in 1909, put it this way: 'The social organization [of these people] ... has been greatly broken up during the past half century ... [Although] their winter camps usually contain several related families, clans ... now have no importance whatever.'[21] In short, at the turn of the century the Fort Hope Indians were a loosely knit confederacy of small family groups, and it was with these people that the Dominion of Canada opened up treaty negotiations in order to gain access to valuable northern resources such as minerals and timber.[22]

The James Bay Treaty

The treaty that brought the Fort Hope people under the jurisdiction of the Canadian government was part of the James Bay Treaty, or Treaty No 9. It was signed at the Hudson's Bay Company post at Fort Hope on the afternoon of 19 July 1905. Under the terms of the treaty the band was promised a reserve, and each person was given eight dollars in cash. The people were also told that they each would receive four dollars per year as long as they maintained their Indian status.[23] According to the treaty commissioners all went well when the treaty was signed, except for a few minor misconceptions that were easily cleared up.[24]

Today some band members are bitter about the treaty. As one of them told us:

When the [commissioners from the] government came here, the people already knew that other treaties were signed. But you have to remember they still didn't know much about what was happening. Here was the government promising all kinds of things, like a reserve and annuity payments, and all the people had to do was promise their allegiance to the King.

But of course they didn't know the full implications, and there's little doubt about that. They didn't know they were signing away all their land for a reserve the government would control anyway, and they certainly didn't know the annuity payment, which was worth a lot of money then, would be worth nothing today.

No! The people didn't know anything about that, and today, almost everyone in the band knows they got ripped off, whether they are honest enough to admit it or not.

Still, it would be unreasonable to suppose that the chiefs who signed the treaty were acting in ignorance. In 1905 they were in an extremely precarious position. Even the treaty commissioners found it worthwhile to remark that the Fort Hope people 'undoubtedly at times ... suffer from a lack of food owing to the circumstances under which they live.'[25] Given this fact, the decline of the fur trade, and a strong likelihood that white people soon would be entering the area, the chiefs' agreement to the treaty is easier to understand.

The treaty commissioners also promised that the government would not interfere with the band's economy, and for more than fifty years this promise was kept. The only significant change the government recorded for the Fort Hope Band during the first half of this century was an increase in size. In 1906 the population was approximately 500; in 1960 it was 1,000, in 1970 1,500, and today it is almost 2,000, although only about 1,400 people live in the band villages at the present time.

3

Schools, welfare, and the White Paper

The life-style that existed in the band from the time the treaty was signed came to an abrupt end during the 1960s. Since then, the social and economic lives of the people have changed more than anyone could have imagined and almost without question because of two key moves that were made by the federal government. First, after hearing a barrage of complaints from band members that residential schools were destroying their families, the Indian Affairs Branch agreed to build schools near the Hudson's Bay Company posts at Fort Hope, Lansdowne House, and Webequie. Once this happened the people began to settle in what are now their villages, and by the end of the decade they had developed a new political system to cope with the complex problems of managing three rapidly growing settlements. Since village life was inconsistent with trapping, band members also discovered a new way to support themselves. Unfortunately, it was an economy based on welfare and social assistance, and this made the people more dependent on government than at any other time in their history.

The increasing reliance on welfare set the stage for another federal initiative that had an important impact on the band. In 1969, in a rush to redress the serious social and economic wrongs Indian people were facing across the country, the newly elected Liberal government released its White Paper on Indian policy. Since recently discovered evidence indicates that Liberal policy-makers may have been guilty of imitating outdated United States government documents when they designed the White Paper and then applying the contents haphazardly to a completely different situation in Canada, it is impossible to tell whether or not they were acting in good faith. One thing is certain: there is absolutely no doubt that the White Paper resulted in a massive flow of new make-work, job-training, and community-development programs into the Fort Hope Band and many other isolated Indian bands. The problem was that these programs did not strengthen the Indians' economy. Under the new policy dependency has only increased, and this has left the people in the Fort Hope Band more vulnerable to government cut-backs than ever before.

Schools and welfare

Although Treaty No 9 said that the government would provide the band with schools, educational materials, and teachers,[1] this did not happen until more than fifty years after the treaty was signed. Before then the government delegated the responsibility for educating band children to Catholic and Anglican missionaries. On and off during the first half of this century the missionaries tried to establish schools where the people traded, but after a number of unsuccessful attempts, band children were finally sent away to residential schools to receive their formal education. The schools were located in southern towns and were generally large, church-sponsored institutions where Indian children from different bands were required to live for most of the year.

From the standpoint of the clergy and the government, the schools were an excellent way to solve a complex social problem. While young children in the band would be provided with the knowledge they would need to participate in modern Canadian society, their parents and grandparents would be allowed to live out their lives in the wilderness. Given this simple plan, the clergy and the government felt that they would be able to meet their mutual responsibilities and satisfy the band's needs simultaneously.

But the residential system created a serious problem. By keeping parents separated from children, and grandparents from grandchildren, the residential system destroyed the integrity of band families. One band member who was educated at a residential school gave us this summary of her school-days:

I was born on my father's trapline, in a cabin ten miles from Lansdowne House. My mother died soon after I was born.

When I was eight, in the summer, the priest talked to my father. They decided I would go to a residential school in the fall. I was told nothing, though; I guess my father didn't want me to be unhappy.

When the day came for me to go, I still didn't know I was going. My father only told me I was going on a trip, like times before when we had gone around in our canoe, but this time I would be alone.

My father took me by canoe to the mission at Lansdowne. There were already two others girls there, older girls who were going to the residential school too. We waited until a plane came. Then my father put me on the plane and we left.

Later, the plane landed in a big town. There a car picked us up and took us to a train station, where we waited again. After we got on the train, we rode for several hours until we came to a place where another car was waiting. This car took us to the school.

It was dark when we arrived. I hadn't eaten all day, hadn't talked, and many things had happened that made me confused. The only thing that made me sleep was that I knew I was going back home.

The next day I saw the school in the daylight. It was the biggest building I had ever seen – halls, classrooms, and big rooms they called dormitories. I was put in one of these dormitories, the one for little girls. There were thirty beds in it.

At first I couldn't understand what was happening. We were always being lined up, and it seemed everyone spoke a strange language, English and other Indian languages I didn't understand. There were also signs in the halls that said 'NO INDIAN,' and that meant we shouldn't speak our own language so we could learn English faster.

I remember there seemed to be bells everywhere. There was the morning bell at seven, when a nun came into our dormitory clapping her hands. She would make us say prayers, like *Deo Gratias*, on our knees beside our beds. Then there was a bell for breakfast, one for classes at nine, one for ten when we would play outside, one for lunch, and others too. The nun in my class also had a small bell that she rang to signal us when we should stand up and sit down.

I went to that school for three years, and I learned English and religion. Whenever I was home in the summer, though, I asked not to go back. It was the loneliness that hurt me the most. It hurt my father too.

This woman's sad experience was by no means unique. During summer vacation other children in the band pleaded with their parents not to be sent back to residential school in the fall. Their parents were sympathetic. They were just as upset by the long periods of enforced separation, and they started to complain to their Indian agents, at first quietly and then with more force. As a result of their protests a new arrangement was finally worked out. In 1962 Indian Affairs built schools near the Hudson's Bay Company posts at Fort Hope, Lansdowne House, and Webequie.

Schools and villages

The new school had a tremendous impact on the way the people lived. Before the schools were built, band members were still basically nomadic, except in summer, when they would camp near the trading posts. But once the buildings were completed, Indian Affairs warned the people to send their children to school or face the consequences, including the threat that family-allowance payments would be stopped. As one of the band's Indian agents who was there at the time explained, permanent communities and a sedentary life-style were the results:

Up until the 1960s a lot of these people didn't live in what are now their present communities. Although there were some small settlements in the area, most of the Indians lived out in the bush on their traplines, and once in a while they would come to the Bay for flour, lard, and tea. Then they would leave again for another three or four months.

But when the modern educational system was established, we told the band they would have to send their kids to school because this was a requirement under the law. We told them they could be penalized if they didn't comply, and so they established permanent settlements near the schools.

What this agent failed to add was that government threats were not the only reason permanent settlements came into being. Since village life allowed the people to reunite their families, another likely reason band members were willing to remain in one place was to restore the intimate family relationships that the residential school system had destroyed.

Schools and political organization

As the villages grew around the schools, the band's political system also began to change. People who were used to living in small groups were now faced with the problems involved in managing three new communities. One result was that the chief and council began to play a much more active role in administering band affairs. In addition, soon after the villages were formed, regularly scheduled air service was inaugurated, and this brought the band into closer contact with the outside world. Federal and provincial officials began to visit much more frequently, and within a short period of time band members were dealing with an ever-increasing number of professional bureaucrats and government programs. For instance, in 1966 Indian Affairs started a housing program to offset shortages in accommodation, but this raised an even more sensitive issue since the people were immediately forced to decide who should be housed first.

To solve the problem, the band created a housing committee, and it decided that the largest families should get houses first. As other problems presented themselves, other committees were struck, and within only a few years each of the band communities had a housing committee, an education committee, a health committee, a planning committee, and a recreation committee. On the advice of their Indian agents the chief and council also agreed to hire a full-time band manager to help them administer band affairs. He started work in 1966 and became the first in a long line of the band's own bureaucrats. Later, as contact increased, still other changes were made, including the election of settlement chairmen and councils in Webequie and Lansdowne House. Altogether these changes meant that by the beginning of the 1970s the people were being governed by a hastily constructed government geared to sedentary life and to interacting with federal and provincial officials.

Schools and the economy

The schools also had an important impact on the band's economy. Before they were built, band members acquired almost all of their spending money by selling their furs to the Bay. But once the schools were opened, the men in the band were faced with an unprecedented conflict. They could continue to work their traplines away from their families, or they could remain in the settlements and look for a different source of income. Given the opportunity to reunite their families so soon after the unpleasant experience of the residential system, the majority chose to remain.

The impact on trapping was devastating. By the mid-1960s the band's production of furs had become erratic, and by the end of the decade it was on a downward spiral (see Figure 1).[2] One government official who had worked in the area for a long time even told us that the band's production of furs was kept at artificially high levels during the 1960s because of the Hudson's Bay manager in charge of the posts at Fort Hope and Lansdowne House. This man allegedly forced men in the villages to trap by withholding government cheques until he was satisfied with production.[3] Under these conditions it is almost certain that the decline in

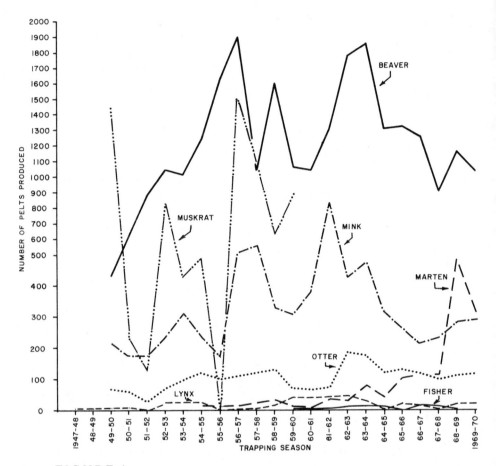

FIGURE 1
Fur harvest in the Fort Hope Band, 1949 through 1970

trapping can be attributed directly to the schools, and this was something the Indian Affairs Branch had not anticipated.

The Branch also failed to consider that, as the men turned away from trapping, they would be forced to rely on government since there was little work to be had in the settlements. For almost sixty years the government had limited its cash payments to band members to three main areas: first, there was the small, four-dollar annuity guaranteed by Treaty No 9[4]; second, starting in 1927, band members seventy years of age and older began to receive an old-age pension up to a maximum of $240 per year; and third, starting in 1946, parents of school-age children began to receive a monthly family allowance up to a maximum of eight dollars per child.[5] Otherwise, virtually all of the government benefits that the people received came in the form of goods and services that were distributed by Indian Affairs.

However, in 1965, at the same time that trapping was declining, the band began to receive welfare and social-assistance payments in cash, including family benefits from the province for the physically and mentally disabled and general welfare assistance from Indian Affairs for the unemployed. The result was startling. By 1969 more than 52 per cent of the people's disposable income came from these two new sources, and in 1969 their disposable income was approximately $679,000. Unfortunately, the government soon would be supplying band members with almost 90 per cent of their disposable income, although this time schools, permanent settlements, and welfare were not the cause. The federal government was about to take a tremendous gamble with Indian people, including the people in the Fort Hope Band.

The White Paper

The origin of the government's second major intrusion into band affairs was the result of a new national concern with Indians. In 1968 Canadians elected a majority Liberal government committed to what incoming Prime Minister Trudeau termed 'The Just Society.' In practical terms this commitment led to the creation of a number of new policies geared to eliminating economic disparities between different regions and peoples in the country, including a new policy for Indians that was outlined in the White Paper released in 1969.

Taking into account the criticisms that had been made in the Hawthorn Report, the White Paper said that the Trudeau government was prepared to offer Canadian Indians economic and political independence. For instance, in the foreword to the paper the government confidently stated that its policy would 'lead to the full, free and non-discriminatory participation of the Indian people in Canadian society. Such a goal requires a break with the past. It requires that the Indian peoples' role of dependence be replaced by a role of equal status, opportunity and responsibility, a role they can share with all other Canadians.'[6]

Following these introductory remarks the government went on to outline the social and political framework through which the Indians would be liberated:

True equality presupposes that the Indian people have the right to full and equal participation in the cultural, social, economic and political life of Canada.

The government believes that the framework within which individual Indians and bands could achieve full participation requires:

1. that the legislative and constitutional basis of discrimination be removed;
2. that there be positive recognition by everyone of the unique contribution of Indian culture to Canadian life;
3. that services come through the same channels and from the same government agencies for all Canadians;
4. that those who are furthest behind be helped most;
5. that lawful obligations be recognized; [and]
6. that control of Indian lands be transferred to the Indian people.[7]

Finally, the government said that in order to create this framework it was prepared to take the following action:

1. Propose to Parliament that the Indian Act be repealed and take such legislative steps as may be necessary to enable Indians to control Indian lands and acquire title to them.
2. Propose to the governments of the provinces that they take over the same responsibilities for Indians that they have for other citizens in their provinces ...
3. Make substantial funds available for Indian economic development as an interim measure.
4. Wind up that part of the Department of Indian Affairs and Northern Development which deals with Indian affairs. The residual responsibilities for programs in the field of Indian affairs would be transferred to other appropriate federal departments.

In addition, the Government will appoint a Commissioner to consult with the Indians and to study and recommend acceptable procedures for the adjudication of [land] claims.[8]

The Indian reaction

Having made these proposals, the federal government soon became embroiled in a bitter dispute with Indian leaders, who said that their people had been dealt an underhanded blow. The Indian Chiefs of Alberta issued a critical reply called 'The Red Paper'[9]; the British Columbia Indians published a 'Brown Paper,'[10] and the Manitoba Indian Brotherhood expressed its anger in a book called *Wahbung: Our Tomorrows*.[11] In these and other documents the Indians objected to the White Paper in the strongest possible terms. They argued that the Indian Act should not be repealed, or certainly not until the question of outstanding land claims was settled. They attacked the provision calling for the delivery of services to all Canadians through the same agencies on the grounds that, while Indians were being shuffled from department to department, DIAND would simply ignore their problems. They also argued that the proposed changes were only a political manoeuvre to allow the government to renege on its treaty obligations.[12] Finally, they objected to the document on the grounds that it had been written and released without any prior consultation. In short, there was little faith in the proposals contained in the White Paper and an almost unanimous rejection of the document by Indian spokesmen.

The government's counter-attack

The government countered these arguments by saying that the White Paper had been grossly misinterpreted. For example, on 1 December 1969 Jean Chrétien, then minister of Indian Affairs, defended the government's new policy in Parliament. In response to a pointed question from an opposition back-bencher, he replied:

The Statement said that the Government would develop, with the Indian people, programs to enrich their cultural heritage and their sense of identity.

How can these proposals be taken as an abrogation of Treaties? Do they sound like cultural genocide? I do not see how anyone can suggest that they are.

As soon as the policy proposal was made public, there were headlines about 'turning the Indians over to the provinces.'

Shortly after the headlines, there were editorials about the problems involved in doing that which was never suggested should be done.

At the same time some Indian leaders began telling the Government it ought not to do that which many of them had sought for years.[13]

Concurrent Resolution 108

Unfortunately, White Paper critics lacked a particularly damning piece of evidence in their dispute with the government – House concurrent Resolution 108, passed by a joint session of the United States Congress on 1 August 1953. Its wording is remarkably similar to that of the White Paper. It reads as follows:

Whereas it is the policy of Congress, as rapidly as possible, to make the Indians ... [in] the United States subject to the same laws and entitled to the same privileges and responsibilities as ... other citizens of the United States, to end their status as wards of the United States, and to grant them all of the rights and prerogatives of American citizenship; and

Whereas the Indians ... [in] the United States should assume their full responsibilities as American citizens: Now, therefore be it

Resolved by the House of Representatives (the Senate concurring), That it is declared to be the sense of Congress that, at the earliest possible time, all of the Indian tribes and the individual members thereof located within the States of California, Florida, New York, and Texas ... should be freed from Federal supervision and control and from all disabilities and limitations specially applicable to Indians ... It is further declared to be the sense of Congress that, upon the release of such tribes and individual members thereof from such disabilities and limitations, all offices of the Bureau of Indian Affairs ... whose primary purpose was to serve any Indian tribe or individual Indian freed from Federal supervision should be abolished. It is further declared to be the sense of Congress that the Secretary of the Interior should examine all existing legislation dealing with such Indians, and treaties between the Government of the United States and each such tribe, and report to Congress at the earliest practicable date, but not later than January 1, 1954, his recommendations for such legislation as, in his judgement, may be necessary to accomplish the purpose of this resolution.[14]

The enabling and subsequent legislation that followed the resolution is also remarkably similar to statements contained in the White Paper.[15] So too are the recommendations of an American task force on Indian Affairs, which reported to President John F. Kennedy in 1961 that the Bureau of Indian Affairs should try to achieve:

1. Maximum Indian economic self-sufficiency.
2. Full participation of Indians in American life.
3. Equal citizenship privileges and responsibilities for Indians.[16]

Had White Paper critics been aware of these striking similarities between the Liberals' new Indian policy and American documents dating back to the early days of the Eisenhower administration, they might also have been aware of just how severely the American policy had been criticized. For instance, John Collier, the American commissioner of Indian Affairs from 1933 to 1945, said bluntly that his government was renewing a 'Century of Dishonor.'[17] He also made this damaging statement about the results of the policy:

On the one hand, Indian property rights were assaulted or destroyed, Indian tribal and community life was disrupted, and the Indians were demoralized and disoriented, not 'assimilated'; on the other hand, administrative absolutism over Indians was intensified and multiplied, the Indian Bureau's drafts upon the Treasury increased instead of diminishing, special interests profited from the removal of [the Indians' special status], the one serious bulwark protecting the Indians' property, and in many instances the Federal Government laid itself open to claims far exceeding the cost of meeting their obligations to the Indians.[18]

Perhaps if Collier's conclusions had been brought before Parliament and to the attention of the Canadian public, the Trudeau government might have abandoned its White Paper proposals. Instead, three important parts of the policy were implemented: a commissioner was appointed to settle Indian claims; massive amounts of money were made available for Indian economic development; and a number of government departments began to provide their services to Indian people for the first time.

By taking these steps, especially the last two, the government was embarking on a course that would see the creation of a new social and economic order among Canada's Indians. Ostensibly, the new order was intended to promote their cultural and economic independence, but for the people in the Fort Hope Band as well as for those in many other bands, the results were exactly the opposite.

DIAND programs

The Fort Hope Band began to experience the impact of the White Paper almost as soon as it was released. DIAND initiated the process with a flurry of new programs. Based on the rationale that jobs would have to be created to remove band members from the welfare rolls and make them economically independent, DIAND's district office in Geraldton spent more than $500,000 to establish and operate sawmills, fisheries, and tourist camps. Make-work projects were started; people were hired to do odd jobs, and the band was given more money for administrative positions. For instance, even as late as 1968 the only full-time administrative officers in the band were the chief and band manager, whereas by 1975 the number had increased to eight, including three new office employees, one social counsellor, one economic-development adviser, and one constable. Together these people were responsible for administering funds in excess of one million dollars per year. Since then socio-economic research staff have been added, and until the building burned in the fall of 1981, all of these people worked out of a new, two-storey band office located in the village of Fort Hope.

Manpower programs

Following hard on the heels of the White Paper, the Department of Manpower and Immigration also became involved in band affairs. In line with DIAND's emphasis on economic development, Manpower began to offer Basic Training for Skills Development (BTSD) courses in the communities to upgrade the people to a grade-eight level in English, arithmetic, and science. As a Manpower official told us:

We became involved with the Fort Hope Band in 1969, at the request of the district superintendent of Indian Affairs.

Before then we were dealing primarily with Indians from reserves in southern Ontario. Our job there was to prepare them to leave the reserve, to give them a portable skill so they could earn a living in the city.

But when we came to Fort Hope, since most of the people were illiterate, we concentrated on BTSD.

BTSD was extremely popular with the people, so much so that between 1969 and 1975 Manpower offered twenty-two of these courses in the villages. This was done at an estimated cost of over one million dollars, much of it going to pay the training allowances of course participants. While it was promoting BTSD, Manpower also spent an additional $500,000 to provide the band with fourteen Canada Manpower Training Program (CMTP) courses, ranging from operating heavy equipment to typing (see Table 1). During the 1970s the department also began to give the band money for community-development projects, first under the auspices of its Local Initiatives Projects (LIP) and Opportunities for Youth (OFY) program and later under similar programs with different names. By 1975 almost $500,000 had been spent on these programs, and again much of it went to the people.

TABLE 1
BTSD and CMTP courses held in the Fort Hope Band 1969–75

Year	Course title	Number enrolled	Number of weeks in course	Location Fort Hope	Lansdowne House	Webequie
1969–70	BTSD	25	24	X		
	BTSD	28	24			X
	CMTP	15	14	X		
	CMTP	15	12	X		
1970–71	BTSD	15	24	X		
	BTSD	15	24		X	
	BTSD	15	24			X
	CMTP	15	12	X		
1971–72	BTSD	13	24	X		
	BTSD	25	24		X	
	BTSD	10	24			X
1972–73	BTSD	32	24	X		
	BTSD	11	24		X	
	BTSD	7	22		X	
	BTSD	2	18		X	
	BTSD	20	24			X
	CMTP	10	14	X		
	CMTP	16	12			X
1973–74	BTSD	30	24	X		
	BTSD	20	24		X	
	BTSD	9	12		X	
	BTSD	31	24			X
	BTSD	3	13			X
	CMTP	15	20		X	
	CMTP	15	20		X	
	CMTP	15	14		X	
	CMTP	9	3		X	
1974–75	BTSD	30	27	X		
	BTSD	20	24		X	
	BTSD	8	24		X	
	BTSD	30	24			X
	CMTP	15	24	X		
	CMTP	12	24	X		
	CMTP	15	11			X
	CMTP	15	8			X
	CMTP	12	20			X
Totals	36	593	708	12	13	11

Other agencies quickly followed DIAND's and Manpower's lead. From 1969 through 1975 the band received funds from the Department of the Environment, the Department of National Health and Welfare, the Department of Public Works, the Secretary of State, the Treasury Board, and the Ontario ministries of Culture and Recreation, Natural Resources, and Transportation and Communications. In fact, by 1975 the number of government programs underway in the band had long since reached the point where bookkeeping and paperwork had become major and tedious chores.

Dependency reaffirmed

From a political standpoint these measures may have been undertaken to show the people in the band that they could acquire the same government benefits as other Canadians. But when agencies such as DIAND and Manpower started to pay band members educational and training allowances and hire them on a part-time and full-time basis, they did not make them economically independent. Although total government investment (that is, welfare and social assistance and job-training and creation) accounted for 64 per cent of the band's disposable income in 1969, in 1975 it accounted for almost 90 per cent.

To make matters worse, poverty was still a major problem. True enough, the band's disposable income had more than doubled between 1969 and 1975, up from less than $700,000 to more than 1.4 million. But by 1975 there were almost 200 more people in the villages than the 1,000 living there in 1969, so that per capita income only increased from $713 to $1,229. During the same two years the corresponding figures for other Canadians were $2,913 and $5,930.[19]

But even more important was the source of this income. In 1969 welfare and social assistance were the mainstay of the band's economy, whereas in 1975 it was short-term programs and steady government jobs – all associated with the White Paper in one way or another. But unlike welfare and social assistance, White Paper initiatives can be withdrawn without notice, and this meant that the band actually became more vulnerable to cut-backs in government funding than it had been before. As for today, judging from discussions with government and band officials, the situation is unchanged. Not surprisingly, band members call the government agents who control the disbursement of funds 'shuniah-ogama,' which literally means money-boss.

Elsewhere

Nor was the Fort Hope experience an isolated event. Elsewhere in the country Indian people were being bombarded with White Paper programs with the same unhappy results. During the 1970s federal expenditures for Indian adult education increased from 84 million dollars to 242 million; expenditures on economic-development programs went up from 40 million to 86 million, and expenditures on job-creation increased from 1.4 million to almost 30 million.[20] Despite all of this spending, the economic prospects of Canada's Indians remain abysmal. The National Indian Brotherhood put it this way in a recent presentation to the Parliamentary Task Force on Employment Opportunities for the 1980s: 'The inescapable conclusion which one must reach is that as matters now stand, Indian people face a future which promises little aside from wider impoverishment and greater dependency.'[21] The presentation also made it clear that this economic dilemma was due 'to the shortcomings of federal policies.'[22]

To us, what is doubly disappointing about the situation is that those responsible for the White Paper have never been willing to admit that key parts of the policy were implemented. Less than two years after the policy was announced, Jean Chrétien told an audience at Queen's University: 'The Government put forward its proposals for a future Indian Policy a year and a half ago. These stimulated and focused a debate and have served a necessary purpose. They are no longer a factor in the debate. *The Government does not intend to force progress along the directions set out in the Policy proposals of June 1969* [emphasis in the original].'[23]

4

Where means became ends

In 1975, when we walked through the band villages for the first time, we saw an unusually large number of young men loitering in small groups. Most were single, between eighteen and twenty-five, and when we talked to them we found out that they were chronically unemployed. They told us that the only opportunity they had to earn any money was by working part-time for government, and this meant participating in a make-work, job-training, or community-development program. They joked with us that White Paper programs were their jobs. Otherwise, they were out of work and on welfare. Even hunting and trapping were beyond their reach since schools had deprived them of the knowledge they needed to live off the land.

The young men were only part of the unemployed. Older, married men, usually with large families to support, also relied on White Paper programs, and when those programs ended, as they always did, these men too had to join the ranks of the unemployed and go on welfare until a new program was offered. To supplement their income most of these men hunted and trapped, and even though they rarely were seen hanging around the villages, they appeared almost as though by magic when a new program was announced. So did women who otherwise always seemed to be busy at home.

Another thing we noticed about the villages was that they lacked most of the community services white people take for granted. None had running water or sewage disposal, and only Fort Hope had electricity for houses. The lack of amenities was reflected in the way the people lived.

The lack of running water, for instance, produced the almost archaic but commonplace scene of women and young girls walking down to the lake in summertime to fill their buckets and cart them home, and in winter of husbands and fathers driving slow-moving snowmachines pulling sleds heavily laden with pails, buckets, and sometimes an old oil drum filled to the brim with water taken from some distant hole where the men had chopped through the ice. The lack of water also meant that mundane chores such as washing clothes were major events, especially in winter when temperatures of −20 and −30 degrees centigrade were not uncommon. Buckets had to be filled, carried home, emptied into washtubs, clothes scrubbed and then hung out to dry on ice-coated binder twine where they would freeze. Washing walls and floors was out of the question. Even getting water for baths, cooking, and drinking was a time-consuming chore, although there was no choice.

The lack of electricity in Lansdowne House and Webequie was a hardship as well since it meant using wood or kerosene for cooking and heating. If wood was used, it had to be cut and split. If the fuel was kerosene, which was also used in lamps, there was the constant danger of a flash fire that no one could extinguish.

The lack of a sewer system led to other problems. It meant not only that people had to use privies but that almost without fail, every spring in each village, excrement and urine would seep into the lake and pollute the water supply. Then, for a week or two or perhaps a month, there would be an unusually high incidence of stomach flu, colds, and diarrhea – not a problem to be taken lightly since it kept adults away from what work there was and children out of school.

The lack of adequate housing was also obvious: ten or twelve people living in a small, drafty, wood-frame house was not uncommon. Nor were there any visible signs of wealth – no fancy furniture, no high-fashion apparel, no new currency in circulation, and, of course, no banks or other financial institutions.

It was clear that we were with a very disadvantaged group of people; we immediately asked ourselves why they stayed instead of moving south, and later, when we found out about their economy, why they found White Paper programs so attractive. The answers to these questions, we discovered, were closely related and led us to conclude that, while government intended its White Paper initiatives to be a means to an end, the people saw them in a completely different light. From their standpoint, because White Paper programs produced immediate social and economic benefits, they were an end in and of themselves.

Money is important

Money was one benefit derived from White Paper programs. For instance, between 1969 and 1975 the cash allowances people in the villages received for participating in the government's new make-work, job-training, and community-development programs rose from $60,438 to $426,577 (see Figure 2).[1] Since in 1975 items such as a loaf of bread cost $1 in the villages and 4 litres of mixed gasoline $2.75, the new money was tremendously important. Without it snowmachines, motorboats, and perhaps even rifles would have been too expensive to buy. As one man told us:

Today the world is very changed from what it once was, not only for Indian people but for everyone.

In the old days we lived off the land, but this is no longer possible. Today everyone is involved with everyone else, and this means we all have to have money.

Money is the common denominator, and since we get most of our money from government programs, we depend on the government to survive.

This man was not exaggerating. In 1975 virtually every household in the band depended on the government for most of its income, and almost 35 per cent of the households, a total of 75, depended on short-term White Paper programs alone (see Table 2).

TABLE 2
Main source of annual income in the Fort Hope Band 1975

Main source of annual income	Number of households	Per capita income							
		$0–499		$500–999		$1,000–1,499		$1,500 +	
		No %		No	%	No	%	No	%
Steady job[a]	45	0	0	5	11	16	36	24	53
Make-work, job-training, and community-development programs	75	7	9.3	49	65.3	16	21.3	3	4
Welfare and social-assistance programs	94	8	8.5	39[b]	41.5	22	23.5	25	26.5[c]
Hunting, trapping, and fishing	5	3	60	1	20	1	20	0	0

[a]Most of these jobs are government jobs.
[b]These households derived most of their income from welfare.
[c]These households derived most of their income from pensions.

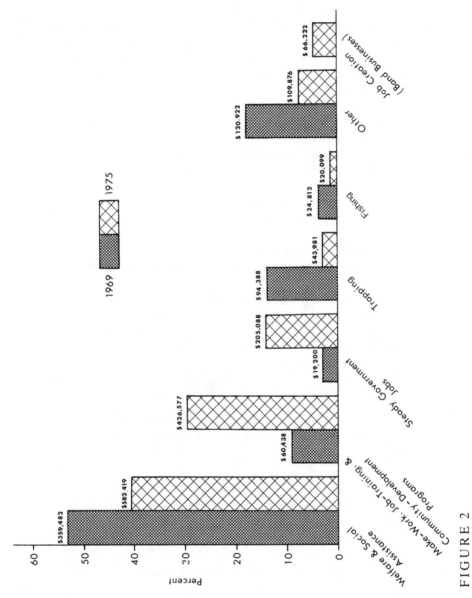

FIGURE 2
Sources and amounts of disposable income in the Fort Hope Band, 1969 and 1975

Administrative effort

The financial importance of the government's new programs is not something that band administrators take lightly. Since make-work, job-training, and community-development programs can be withdrawn at the government's pleasure, the chief, council, and band manager must be aware of the government's intentions, all the more so because budget constraints prevent government agencies from delivering all of their White Paper programs to every community in northern Ontario at the same time. Bands must compete for the programs each year, not only with each other but sometimes also with white communities, and this calls for delicate and complicated negotiations with government officials, sometimes in the north but more often in plush government boardrooms in cities such as Toronto and Ottawa.

Because of the competition for programs, Fort Hope administrators must spend a great deal of time away from home. They must also be able to deal with political pressure. A former band manager put it to us this way:

I worked for the band for three and a half years, and during that time I was under constant pressure.

The government people I dealt with never seemed to be satisfied. They always told me I should be doing more to keep them informed, especially writing reports. They also kept me moving around, sending me from one meeting to another until I was away from home almost as much as I was there.

There were other pressures too, because if I didn't go to a meeting or gave a bad presentation, then there was a good chance the program we were trying to get would be given to some other community, and this meant the people in the band would start to complain because they thought I wasn't doing my job.

In the end I was working twelve hours a day just to keep up, and that was every day of the week.

Other administrative officers in the band told us much the same story. They said that in the beginning they found travelling and dealing with government exciting but that 'sooner or later you realize you're in a big rat race, and when that happens you get fed up and quit.' This has led to some awkward moments in negotiations, say when a chief or band manager resigns, but with capable people filling the gaps, DIAND, Manpower, and other government programs have appeared in the communities with consistent regularity, and band officials know that this has helped keep the economy alive.

So too have steady government jobs, which also appeared as a result of the government's new policy. For instance, in 1968 there were only 10 steady jobs available in the villages – 8 with the Hudson's Bay Company and 2 with the government. But by 1975, although the Bay still employed 8 local people as clerks, the number employed full-time by government had jumped to 37 – 23 in Fort Hope, 8 in Lansdowne House, and 6 in Webequie. And even though most of the new jobs were low-status positions such as janitor, teacher's aide, and nurse's aide,[2] they had an enormous impact on the economy. Between 1969 and 1975 the income acquired from steady government jobs in the band increased from less than $20,000 to more than $200,000 (see Figure 2).

Band administrators understand these relationships all too well. But they told us quite frankly that they were not trying to bring in White Paper programs and acquire steady government jobs because of any deep-seated commitment to the Liberal government or its Indian policy. Nor did they say that they were after the education, training, or community improvements the programs and jobs were intended to provide, although some saw these as fringe benefits. From their standpoint the most important, tangible benefit was money.[3]

Some work is better than no work

Work was another benefit the band gained from White Paper programs. When the people settled in villages, the majority had little to occupy their time, and this was unsettling because they had always worked before. But when the schools were opened they could find no effective way to support themselves except for welfare and social assistance, and this meant that they did not have to work at all. They received money simply because they occupied a specific legal status: reaching sixty-five years of age for old-age pension, becoming a parent for family allowance, having a physical or mental disability for family benefits, and being unemployed for general welfare assistance. The White Paper turned this situation around, especially for those on social assistance.

The best example of the change that took place is the way that band members reacted to the short-term employment opportunities that came their way via programs such as BTSD, CMTP, LIP, OFY, Canada Works, Young Canada Works, and, more recently, Canada Community Development projects, Canada Community Services projects, and Summer

Canada Student Employment programs. When band members participate in these programs, some work always is involved, usually studying or performing a task such as constructing roads, clearing brush, building houses, or even teaching children how to swim. The same is true of other government programs such as tree-planting and fire-fighting for the Ministry of Natural Resources. If anyone enrolled in these programs is unable or unwilling to work, the band's job-selection committee finds a replacement immediately, although government officials told us that replacements rarely are needed since completion rates for the programs are higher than 80 per cent.

Equally important, by 1975 these short-term White Paper programs were threatening to overtake welfare and social assistance as the single most important source of disposable income in the band. In 1969, make-work, job-training, and community-development programs accounted for just under 9 per cent of the band's disposable income, and welfare and social assistance just over 52 per cent. But only six years later, welfare and social assistance had dropped to 40 per cent while short-term programs had jumped to 30 per cent. In other words, while welfare and social assistance declined by more than 12 per cent in relation to other sources of income, short-term government programs increased by more than 20 per cent.

Given this pattern, the question that comes to mind is whether the people in the Fort Hope Band have been participating in the short-term programs because they would rather work than have nothing to do. Since the income they get from welfare and the new programs is roughly the same, the answer is almost certainly yes. In fact, in some cases band members can actually acquire more money from general welfare assistance and family benefits than they can from BTSD and CMTP (see Table 3). And those on welfare would have been free to do other things. Yet people still participate in the programs, even though they cannot collect welfare at the same time.

Nor is it likely that band members were attracted to short-term White Paper programs to meet the aims of government planners from the south. Take the case of Manpower's BTSD and CMTP courses.[4] Again looking at the period from 1969 to 1975, Manpower spent over 1.5 million dollars to provide the band with 36 courses, which almost 600 people completed, including more than 150 in 1975 alone. But while these courses were designed to prepare band members for subsequent employment in the modern Canadian economy, the Manpower officials we talked to admitted that the department had achieved an entirely different result. The courses

TABLE 3
Maximum benefits acquired from different government programs

Programs	Maximum monthly allowance for			
	One adult	With one dependent	Two dependents	Three dependents
Family benefits[a]	$218	$387	$459	$520
General welfare assistance[b]	$222	$447	$457	$519
BTSD and CMTP[c]	$280	$360	$420	$480

[a]Ontario *The Family Benefits Act* (Toronto 1979) 64.
[b]Ontario *The General Welfare Assistance Act* (Toronto 1980) 52.
[c]Canada *The Canada Gazette* pt 2, vol 114, no 18 (Ottawa 1980) 3179.

simply became employment opportunities in and of themselves, just like the majority of make-work, job-training, and community-development programs the White Paper spawned in the band. No wonder the young men we talked to told us that White Paper programs were their jobs.

Why people stay

Since there are more opportunities to earn money and get jobs elsewhere in the country, it stands to reason that these are not the only benefits the people in the band derive from White Paper programs. Another is the chance to keep their communities intact. Because life in the villages is hard, some may think this strange, but even though the communities are certainly no utopia, to the people who live there they are much more than simply places to live. Except for Lansdowne House they are places where people act the same way, speak the same language, think along the same lines, believe in the same things, and share the same goals.

This sense of community is extremely important to the band, as it is almost everywhere. In fact, in a survey we used to sample the opinions of 221 band members, an overwhelming majority indicated that they would much rather live in the villages than in a city or town. While most had been to the south, they said that their own communities were easier to live in, provided them with a better social life, made them feel secure, and let them make friends more easily and raise children better. The only positive thing they had to say about urban life was that it was modern and offered more job opportunities. The people in Lansdowne were the exceptions. They did not evaluate their community highly because of the drinking and violence (see Table 4).

Almost everyone we talked to privately also told us that he or she had no strong desire to leave. A man from Webequie put it this way:

> In Webequie I feel at home, but that's not the way I feel in the south because when I'm there I'm just an Indian and people react in a different way.
>
> You know, sometimes when I want a hotel room they won't rent me one because they say they don't rent rooms to drunken Indians. This has happened to me even when I haven't had a drink, so I end up sleeping down by the railway tracks.

Given the possibility of this kind of reception in the white community, no wonder the attractions of urban life are far outweighed by life in the band.

High-school students

Even teenagers, the most restless group in the band, have a strong sense of community. Although some bragged about how easily they could make it down south, most live in the villages after they quit school. Take the case of high-school students, who go to school not in their own communities but in Geraldton, where DIAND's district office is located. Regrettably, the drop-out rate is exceptionally high, hovering around 50 per cent each year. But according to the DIAND officer who counsels these students, the reason they drop out has nothing to do with 'aptitude' or 'intelligence.' He says that 'homesickness' is the cause, and most of the students we spoke to agreed. As one of them told us:

> I was the first in my family to be sent away to high school and one of the first from Fort Hope. I went with two girls, but both were older so we didn't have much contact.
>
> My first day I was really amazed. I was used to being with my own people, but at the school almost everyone was white. I think there were only ten Indians, and I remember thinking I'd sit with one of them. But everyone ended up in different rooms because we were in different grades or taking different subjects, so I ended up alone, the only Indian in a class of thirty or thirty-five whites, and I was plenty scared.
>
> Finally, it came to the point where I couldn't stand it any more. I knew if I didn't get home I'd go crazy, so I quit school and came back here. Since then I've had my ups and downs, but I still think it was a good decision.

TABLE 4
Sample evaluation of urban and band life-styles (percentages)

	Yes			No[a]		
	F	M	Total	F	M	Total
Have you visited a city or town during the past 12 months? F = 78, M = 94	51	53	52	49	47	48
Is your own community easier to live in than a city? F = 79, M = 97	82	90	86	18	10	14
Does your own community provide you with a better social life than a city? F = 75, M = 97	76	83	80	24	17	20
Does your own community provide you with more security than a city? F = 74, M = 95	80	87	84	20	13	15
Does living in your own community allow you to make friends more easily than living in a city? F = 78, M = 96	71	74	73	29	26	27
Does living in your own community allow you to raise children better than living in a city? F = 79, M = 94	51	50	51	49	50	49
Does your own community provide you with more modern conveniences than a city? F = 73, M = 91	29	36	28	71	64	72
Does your own community provide you with more job opportunities than a city? F = 76, M = 95	24	14	19	76	86	81

[a]The majority of negative responses are from Lansdowne House.

For this student and others who drop out the cost of coming home is almost-certain unemployment. Most are forced to go on welfare, but for a few lucky ones there is a White Paper program. And even though they are no better off in terms of dependency, at least they have something to take up their time.

The missing ingredient

An economy based on government hand-outs is not attractive to the band for obvious reasons, no matter how high a value they place on community life. They are still desperately poor. But if White Paper programs and steady government jobs were withdrawn, the people would be even poorer – worse, they would have nothing to do and probably nowhere to go. In that sense the government's new policy has been a dismal failure; it has not freed the band, only made it more dependent and more subject to government control.

Although the people in the band talk about economic independence a great deal, only the most optimistic believe that they will be able to turn their economy around. The majority realize that they do not have the votes or political power to change the programs they have come to rely on for their livelihood so that the programs will become a means to an end rather than an end in themselves. And the people in the Fort Hope Band are not the only ones who are caught up in this economic dilemma. According to a recent report by the National Indian Socio-Economic Development Committee, Indian people throughout the country have shared the same fate:

While statistics point to ever-increasing expenditures by Government and greater quantities of physical assets and available services, statistics also confirm the fact that Indian people have lost control over their lives ... *The tragedy is that there is no evidence of improvement in this intolerable condition in spite of increasing Government expenditures.*

Many attempts have been made to explain this desolate situation ... Whatever the preferred doctrine, it can be concluded that the contemporary crisis ... [is] rooted in ... [the] limitation of human freedom [emphasis in the original].[5]

As the next two chapters will show, a lack of freedom to control their own affairs was one of the main reasons behind the failure of the government's attempts to establish successful businesses in the band.

5

Why band businesses failed

Make-work, job-training, and community-development programs were not the only means the government used in its attempt to revitalize the economy of the Fort Hope Band. During the 1970s DIAND also tried to start a number of businesses in the communities, including three fishing co-operatives, two sawmills, two tourist camps, and a co-op store. But when we looked at the businesses, we found that none had succeeded. Nor did it seem likely that any of them would,[1] and this was disheartening to everyone concerned, not just because DIAND had spent well over 1.5 million dollars to establish the businesses but also because things actually looked quite promising at the start.

Four lost opportunities

The fishing co-operatives

For instance, when fisheries were created for the people in Fort Hope, Webequie, and Lansdowne, the situation seemed ideal. Each co-operative employed an average of six full-time and fifteen part-time fishermen who fished for pickerel and whitefish from the beginning of June until the end of August. Groups of two or three fishermen would set up a base camp on a large lake and fish that one as well as one or two others nearby. When a load of fish was ready for market, a small plane would be sent in to pick up the catch and deliver any supplies the fishermen needed. The men also used the plane to return home to visit their wives and children, each man taking a turn until the end of June, when school was let out and their families could join them. From then until the end of the

TABLE 5
Number of commercial fishermen in the Fort Hope Band and their distribution in terms of net earnings 1970 and 1976

		1970	1976
No of commercial fishermen in the band		83	60
Total amount earned		$62,700	$27,443
Average per capita earnings		$ 755	$ 457
Distribution in terms of net earnings			
$0–500	No	30	40
	%	36	67
$500–1,000	No	28	12
	%	34	20
$1,000 +	No	25	8
	%	30	13

summer the camps became small communities, with wives and children close at hand assisting the men while they worked at netting fish. The record of each fisherman's production was kept by DIAND's district office, and when the men returned home at the end of the summer, each would be paid according to how much he had produced for the co-operative as a whole.

Since there was no shortage of fish in any of the lakes, high production and profits seemed to be assured, so DIAND began to invest heavily in the fisheries. From 1969 through 1975 the department spent $250,000 on docks, fishing sheds, ice houses, ice-making equipment, two-way radios, and nets. In addition, since DIAND felt that the fishermen needed business advice, field advisers were sent in to help them learn ways of cutting costs and increasing profits. Yet consistently and without fail, year after year, the production of fish dropped and the number of fishermen declined. Between 1970 and 1977 the fisheries' total production fell from more than 100,000 kilograms to less than 40,000 kilograms. At the same time the number of full-time fishermen dropped from 25 to 8 and the number of helpers from 58 to 52 (see Table 5). To complicate matters, the few men who continued to fish often acted as though they had absolutely no interest in what happened to the new equipment that DIAND had bought – nets were lost, two-way radios misplaced, and ice-making equipment ignored.

The sawmills

The sawmills in Fort Hope and Webequie fared no better, despite a $170,000 investment by DIAND. The sawmills were built to supply the lumber needed for housing construction in the two villages, and since the number of new houses to be built was determined by the department a year ahead of time, it was assumed that there would be no problem in turning a profit in the sawmills. But by the mid-1970s there were a staggering number of problems – too many workers had been hired, at times twice the number required, and this made the mills unprofitable; inventory was not controlled; records were not kept properly; and an effective management system was never established. The result was general confusion and chronic shortages of working capital. A 1976 DIAND report on the financial status of the sawmill in Webequie put it this way:

The sawmill continues to experience financial problems and was out of capital by the middle part of July. The main problem is that although the sawmill should operate at a profit, ... it never has any capital. Last year, for example, housing material for four houses disappeared by the time ... [the people] started building [houses] in the spring ... No one seems to know where this material went. The records for 1975 were incomplete. Few records of the transactions between the sawmill and various individuals in the community are kept. In addition, the Bay acts as the bank so it is impossible to check deposits or withdrawals, etc. Without adequate capital, the sawmill cannot cut lumber for next year's construction. Yet, the lumber must be cut one year in advance to allow it to dry.[2]

The tourist camps

The situation in the tourist camps appeared to be much the same as in the other band businesses (see Table 6). Depending on the year, each camp consisted of four or five fly-in sites situated near Fort Hope and Webequie, but even after DIAND invested a good deal of money, including $20,000 in capital equipment alone, neither camp ever produced a profit. This was extremely surprising because there was a large American tourist market, particularly in the midwest in cities such as Minneapolis and Chicago, and the lakes and rivers in the area offered some of the best pickerel and trout fishing on the continent. Under the circumstances it seemed as though all that had to be done to make the camps succeed was to work out attractive packages at competitive rates, advertise, make sure

TABLE 6

The economic status of DIAND-supported businesses in the Fort Hope Band at the end of 1975

	Fishery	Sawmill	Tourist camp	Totals
Fort Hope				
Initial capital cost	$100,000	$125,000	$100,000	$325,000
Amount of subsidy required in 1975	$ 10,000	$ 3,000	$ 5,000	$ 18,000
No of jobs produced in 1975	33	24	18	75
Amount of salaries produced in 1975	$ 10,131	$ 16,374	$ 7,164	$ 33,669
Lansdowne House				
Initial capital cost	$ 75,000	—	—	$ 75,000
Amount of subsidy required in 1975	$ 10,000	—	—	$ 10,000
No of jobs produced in 1975	24	—	—	24
Amount of salaries produced in 1975	$ 6,350	—	—	$ 6,350
Webequie				
Initial capital cost	$ 75,000	$ 45,000	$160,000	$280,000
Amount of subsidy required in 1975	$ 10,000	$ 3,000	$ 5,000	$ 18,000
No of jobs produced in 1975	18	7	49	74
Amount of salaries produced in 1975	$ 3,618	$ 7,738	$ 14,847	$ 26,203

that adequate facilities were built, hire and train local people as guides and cooks, and, most important of all, arrange for a plane to fly in the customers.

DIAND certainly tried. Near Fort Hope and Webequie, small guest cabins were strategically located on the shores of isolated and peaceful lakes teeming with pickerel and northern pike and close to streams offering spectacular trout fishing; boats, motors, and two-way radios were supplied; planes were leased; and band members were trained to guide and cook for tourists and make them feel comfortable. From DIAND's point of view the camps had everything a well-run tourist camp needed to succeed.

But the camps did not succeed. Too many guides were hired; boats and motors were misused and misplaced; cabins were broken into; and finally, as in the sawmills, few records were kept and management was poor. According to an internal DIAND report, the result by the spring of 1975 was that:

No one had looked at the books in a couple of years. The camps were in serious financial difficulty, almost $10,000 in debt ... Equipment was missing and damaged, and there was no accurate inventory to determine what was needed for the coming season. If a cost analysis, or profit and loss statement had been done, they were seriously in error, for using the new rate for the 1976 season we determined that the camps would lose money by operating ...

The co-op store

The co-op store in Fort Hope was just as disappointing. The idea to start the co-op dated back to the summer of 1973, when DIAND officials asked the band council to determine what kind of business the people in Fort Hope wanted for their village. As it turned out, the majority wanted a general store to compete with the Bay. They said that they were tired of seeing the Bay make so much money in their villages, that the company had an unfair credit policy, that it ignored the problems of people on fixed incomes, especially the old, and that the only way these problems could be overcome would be to eliminate the Bay's monopoly.

The band prepared a summary of these comments and passed it on to DIAND's district office. District officials were impressed by the band's arguments and arranged to hire a consultant to conduct a feasibility study – something of a milestone, since this had never been done for any of the other businesses. After conducting his study the consultant concluded that the population of the reserve could support a second store, so he prepared a proposal that endorsed the idea of a new co-op supermarket in the reserve. He decided on a co-op because he felt that the people would be more inclined to shop where they would receive cash returns on their purchases.

After discussing the project with band officials, the district office approved the proposal and passed it on to a higher echelon of DIAND, with a covering letter recommending that a co-op store be built. The district office also sent the proposal to the Indian Community Secretariat (ICS)[3] since there was an informal understanding between DIAND and the ICS that, if the supermarket were built, it would be jointly financed by federal and provincial money. After reviewing the proposal both agencies agreed on its merit, and together they promised the band $160,000 to pay for construction and supplies. But even with this promising start, after a series of misfortunes, by 1979 the co-op was more than $50,000 in debt.

What went wrong?

The performance of the businesses perplexed DIAND. Some departmental officials were angry. As one of the band's business advisers told us:

The facts speak for themselves. The businesses hire too many people to make them profitable, show no regard for budgets, misuse equipment, and in general show terrible business management practices. To boot, the people are lazy, pure and simple, and if it wasn't for us there wouldn't be any businesses.

I think we should stop this sort of needless waste. The best way to teach the band what business is all about is to let them go under when they do. All we're doing by supplying them with funding is telling them that we always will [fund them], no matter what.

But most of the agents we talked to rejected this view. They felt that they should be doing more. The question was, what? If DIAND had failed consistently, how could new ways be found to prevent failure? Perhaps band members had to go through one or two generations before they could grasp the subtleties of twentieth-century business practices?

This was the climate we faced. Needless to say, it was hardly a pleasant starting point. If band members could not succeed in business, it was doubtful that much could be done to provide them with the jobs they said they needed in order to reduce their dependence on government. One point we were certain about. Terms such as 'lazy' served little purpose. They only confused the issue and prevented us from finding effective solutions. With this in mind we tried to find out why band businesses had failed.

A lack of clear and workable objectives

One thing we discovered was that the band's businesses were created during a period when DIAND was trying to set up Indian businesses across the country. The government had committed DIAND to this course in the White Paper.[4] Although the White Paper did not say which businesses DIAND would support, it did say that Indians would require business experience in order for them to achieve their full economic potential. After that it would only be a matter of time until they would be able to integrate themselves into the national economy and begin to enjoy the same economic benefits that were available to other Canadians.

To its credit, the government also admitted that it would be extremely difficult to start businesses in isolated reserves and on Crown land, not just because the people lacked managerial and technical knowledge but because existing legislation made it virtually impossible for bands to pledge land or resources as collateral.[5] As the White Paper noted: 'Even where reserves have economic potential, the Indians have been handicapped. Private investors have been reluctant to supply capital for projects on land which cannot be pledged as security. Adequate social and risk capital has not been available from public services. Most Indians have not had the opportunity to acquire managerial experience, nor have they been offered sufficient technical assistance.'[6] But this problem also could be solved, the White Paper said, by making massive amounts of money available and providing Indians with good advice:

To develop Indian reserves to the level of the regions in which they are located will require considerable capital over a period of some years, as well as the provision of managerial and technical advice ...

In addition, and as an interim measure, the Government is prepared to make substantial additional funds available for investment in the economic progress of the Indian people. This would overcome the barriers to early development of Indian lands and resources, help bring Indians into a closer working relationship with the business community, help finance their adjustment to new employment opportunities, and facilitate access to normal financial services.[7]

DIAND tried to meet these commitments by investing heavily in Indian businesses. During the 1970s the department allocated large sums of money to Indian people in the form of direct loans, guaranteed loans, grants, and contributions. In fact, between 1970 and 1980 the department loaned Indian businesses approximately 250 million dollars under the auspices of its Indian Economic Development Fund, compared to less than 50 million the decade before.[8] DIAND also provided business advice, on its own and through consultants. But by the late 1970s not much had been achieved, and by all accounts, including numerous in-house reports, DIAND's hope of helping Indian people to run successful businesses had failed to materialize.

For instance, in a 1978 report the national management-consulting firm of Hickling-Johnson said that:

The Department's experience in attempting to achieve their objectives over the last five to ten years has been disappointing. Some progress has been made, but studies conducted by departmental consultants and private firms have documented numerous difficulties and over the last two years the Department has been engaged in an effort to rationalize its development efforts. The most publicized aspect of this effort has been the stabilization of the Indian Economic Development Fund.[9]

The extent to which the department was having trouble stabilizing the fund was made public in 1980, when DIAND requested Treasury Board approval to write off seventeen million dollars in outstanding loans to Indian businesses that department officials said they could not collect.[10]

The reasons for DIAND's failure to establish successful businesses are complex, but they all point towards the department's failure to set clear and workable objectives, a fundamental task in any planning exercise. As Hickling-Johnson put it:

Unfortunately, we must report that at the regional and district levels of the Department the policy objectives ... have not provided sufficient guidance as to what DIAND is trying to achieve. The root of the difficulty lies in the absence of a clear definition of economic development itself. The consequence of the difficulty is that the Department is trying to do different, sometimes contradictory, things all at the same time. It is, for example, trying to be a tough-minded lender (to teach Indians a sense of responsibility and expose them to 'commercial reality'), while at the same time it is trying to be understanding and easy-going in recognition of Indians' lack of experience.[11]

The above certainly was true for the Indian agents who worked with the Fort Hope Band. In a number of discussions with DIAND officials at the regional and district level, we were left with the impression that there was confusion and disagreement about what the overall objectives of business development were supposed to be. Some took a hard line and argued that a band business should not be supported if it did not become self-sufficient within a reasonable period of time. Others took a soft approach and argued that economic development could not be separated from social development; if a band business improved the quality of life in a village by creating jobs, they said, then it should be supported regardless of whether it ever became self-sufficient.

Altogether this led to an inconsistent approach, with the department emphasizing first one thing and then another. For instance, between 1969 and 1976 the main thrust of DIAND's business-development strategy was to create jobs in the band, whereas since that time business viability has been the main concern. The same was true with regard to control. During the early 1970s DIAND thought it best if it controlled the businesses, but by 1977 the tourist camps had been turned over to the band and the department was considering turning over the other businesses at some future point. What the criteria were for turning the businesses over remained unknown. The transfers were simply decided upon by someone in the department who thought it was a good idea at the time.

Nor did DIAND establish effective ways to monitor and assess the performance of the businesses for future funding. In our research we were surprised to find absolutely no baseline information available to measure the economic impact of the businesses on the people. Instead, the department spent a great deal of money to create the fisheries, sawmills, tourist camps, and the co-op store, yet no one could tell us if the average worker had improved his earnings from the year before. We were told that no one kept records of that sort. But then, no one could refer to a clear set of objectives that said DIAND should be keeping those records.

In short, DIAND policy-makers did not take the time to work out a set of guidelines that would encourage effective and consistent action on the part of its field staff. All that district officials had to go on were the broad statements of general principle contained in the White Paper. The result was a confused and chaotic approach to business development in the band, marked by mismanagement, an improper use of incentives, and a failure to recognize the crucial role of individual initiative.

Moreover, we discovered early on in our work that the term 'band business' was really a misnomer. The businesses were never owned by the band; they were owned by Indian Affairs. DIAND officials explained the confusion by saying that the department only owned the businesses 'on paper' and only for the short term. As soon as the businesses were profitable and the people had been taught proper management practices, they would be turned over. In the interim, the businesses would be run by Indian managers who would report directly to DIAND. It was thought that eventually the managers might own the businesses, but while the people were learning, the department maintained control, and sometimes it mismanaged more than it managed.

The co-op: a study in mismanagement

The Fort Hope co-op store probably suffered more from departmental mismanagement than any of the other businesses. Although DIAND and the Indian Community Secretariat were committed to the idea for the store in 1973, it was not until the summer of 1975 that plans for the building were finalized. In the meantime, a few people had joined the co-op, a board of directors had been selected, and DIAND became the board's principal adviser.[12]

But DIAND's involvement paralysed the project from the start. For example, when the blueprints for the store were finally approved, instead of calling for tenders to be submitted DIAND simply hired a person from the south to supervise community labour. When this man quit for personal reasons,[13] DIAND concluded that he had gone because the people were working too slowly, and on this assumption the department decided that all future work would be done by outsiders. As a result, three new men from the outside were hired to build the supermarket, but rather than enter into a formal contract with these men the district office left them on their own,[14] which meant that they were free to record, without any departmental supervison, the number of hours they were supposed to have worked. The three proved to be unreliable, and labour costs sky-rocketed. At times they were earning as much as $1,000 a week each, and even after they left Fort Hope they still submitted large overtime claims to the district office for work they allegedly had performed. Nor did the department conduct formal inspections while construction was underway, and when the buildings were completed, work done by the three was found to be faulty and had to be redone – an outside wall was weak and the electrical system was substandard. Independent witnesses also told us that on several occasions the three were too drunk to do any work at all. The police even had to ask one of them to leave the reserve for public drunkenness.[15]

Furthermore, although the original blueprints called for a modest apartment to be built above the store as a residence for the manager, DIAND decided that a separate, two-storey and purposely opulent house with a cathedral ceiling should be built instead. The department's rationale was that the house would be a strong incentive to attract a qualified (white) manager from the south. The fact that it would be the only two-storey house in the reserve and a possible source of conflict was apparently not considered. In any event, the house was used as a residence only for a short time since the cost of heating it and supplying it with power was found to be prohibitive.

The white manager

A much more serious problem arose when a totally inexperienced person was hired to be the store's first manager. Although the board of directors was content to hire a local person for the job, it was not allowed to make this decision on its own. Instead, DIAND assigned one of its Indian agents and a consultant to advise the co-op, and they convinced the board to hire a non-Indian who had little experience with Indians, co-operatives, or retail sales.

They also asked the board to let them monitor the manager's performance, but, as the following excerpt from a DIAND report written after he had resigned shows, not only did the advisers choose a poor manager; they also failed to monitor his performance as they had promised:

The store's initial manager, who had no experience with the retail trade or with Indian communities and, ultimately, with those to whom he was responsible, demonstrated little management skill. The store sat idle for about a month after its scheduled opening in January on the rather lame excuse that there was no cash register. No pre-opening inventory was done, consequently little control of inventory existed. Proper records of sales and disbursements evidently were not kept. Incoming shipments evidently were not checked against invoices and consequently ordered goods could have arrived damaged or not at all without anyone's being aware of it. Claims for goods known to have arrived damaged evidently were not made, and by the time the Indian Affairs adviser instructed the present [Indian] manager to make such claims, it was too late. Records of money received on account apparently were not properly kept, as several customers have told the present manager that they already have paid what appear to be outstanding accounts. A skidoo more suited to racing than freight-hauling was purchased for more than $3,000. Some extraordinary purchases were made for 'promotional' purposes, such as a Polaroid camera, supposed to be used for advertising in a community where no medium for advertising exists.

Another section of the same report was even more damaging. It called the manager's honesty into question:

The store has invoices for a number of goods which cannot be found in the community. The manager is reported to have arrived in Fort Hope with one suitcase and one box ... [but allegedly left with much more]. According to [wholesale] officials, the manager admits to having taken a number of items and has promised to return them to suppliers, but according to the suppliers involved, he had returned nothing by late June [three months after his departure]. Before leaving, the manager did his final cash count in the presence of an airline pilot who flew him out, not in the presence of co-op officials.

The outcome

The result of these extraordinary events was devastating to the co-op. By April 1976 it had spent over $60,000 more than its original $160,000 budget. The new business was suffering from a severe shortage of working capital, and this meant that there was not enough money to pay bills, let alone dividends to co-op members. Suppliers who were owed money became increasingly reluctant to ship stock; the inventory in the store began to dwindle, and the members started to shop at the Bay, where there was a wider selection of goods. There was every indication that, caught in this vicious circle, the co-op was headed for bankruptcy.

Given the seriousness of the situation, the board of directors encouraged the original manager to resign and hired a much more competent man from within the band. On his recommendation all credit sales were discontinued; people with outstanding accounts were asked to bring them up to date; the price of merchandise was raised to maintain an adequate margin of profit; overhead costs were reduced; and an active campaign was initiated to encourage people to shop at the store. When these changes were made, the co-op did begin to show a profit, but long-range forecasts still indicated that it would be years before the co-op would be able to pay off its debts.

Frustrated and disappointed, the board approached DIAND for help, and a compromise was finally worked out. LEAP funds had been allocated to create a new business called the Fort Hope Development Corporation – the largest business the government had ever sponsored in the band. The new corporation was about to open three tourist camps, and its board of directors said that it was interested in buying the now-vacant co-op manager's residence and converting it into an inn with a restaurant. They were willing to pay $50,000 for the building if DIAND would provide them with a loan, and for a short time it looked as though the loan would be approved. But after two months of optimism the bubble burst. Due to LEAP regulations the Fort Hope Development Corporation had been organized as a non-profit enterprise, and this made it ineligible for the DIAND loan it was seeking.

Stopgap help

The co-op's board of directors was back where it had started, and with no place else left to turn to arrange financing for the supermarket, the board approached the chief and council of the band. The band's administration was well aware of the co-op's problems, and after meeting with the board the chief and council agreed to loan the supermarket $10,000. Needless to say, this was only a stopgap measure – co-op debts still totalled $60,000; working capital was practically non-existent, and suppliers began to demand cash payments before shipping merchandise.

The board realized that it could not go on borrowing from the band indefinitely, and in a last-ditch attempt to save the co-op the board decided to renew its efforts to obtain money from DIAND, this time with help from Grand Council Treaty 9,[16] whose lawyer hinted that the co-op might sue DIAND for mismanaging the store. At the same time the newly appointed director general of Indian Affairs in Ontario was made aware of the situation, and he indicated that he was sympathetic to the Indians' cause. In the end, as a result of these manoeuvres and possibly realizing its culpability, DIAND finally did agree to loan the co-op $50,000. The ultimate irony, of course, is that the co-op is still in debt to the agency whose mismanagement resulted in the debt in the first place.

The people's view

To say that the people are bitter about this turn of events is an understatement, despite the fact that the Bay burned down in the fall of 1981 and the co-op now has a monopoly. One person summed things up this way:

The co-op is the way it is today not because of us but because of Indian Affairs. They were the ones who financed it badly; they were the ones who hired the construction crew; and they were the ones who hired the first manager.

These people almost destroyed the co-op, and when the board asked Indian Affairs for help and pointed out how they were responsible, they kept on holding back.

Indian Affairs are also the ones we have to pay back, and will have to pay back for the next twenty years.

They have made it so hard for us that many people are fed up and want to quit. And you know what Indian Affairs will say then? They'll say: 'The Indians are to blame,' but the only thing we can be blamed for is being dumb enough to get screwed.

Minimal incentives

Another problem that hampered band businesses was that they did not provide their employees with sufficient money or work. For instance, although the band acquired more than one million dollars from government in 1975, the people who worked for the fisheries, sawmills, and tourist camps earned only $66,222. This works out to an average annual income of $383 for each of the 173 people who were employed, or around $34 per month. Granted, all of these businesses are seasonal and operate for only four or five months during the spring and summer, but even taking the seasonal factor into account, the average income of the employees was still only about $85 a month. Given this negligible amount, it was simply impossible to attract people to the jobs on a long-term basis, and this meant that the businesses were never able to provide band members with an opportunity to establish careers.

The way DIAND handled the band's three commercial fisheries exemplifies this best. Up until 1969 the policy of the Ministry of Natural Resources was to allocate one commercial fishing licence to each of the band communities.[17] After receiving the licence, the fishermen were allowed to operate on their own and were free to sell their fish on an individual basis at the market price. The purchasing was done by private airlines who bought the fish and transported them south, where they were sold to wholesale and retail firms. Although there were problems with this procedure, particularly because aircraft were not always available to transport the catch, the fishermen were still fairly successful. Even as late as 1966 the Ministry of Natural Resources was able to report that commercial fishing in the band went 'fairly well this season, and the Indian fishermen continue to improve their respective operations each successive year.'

But when the White Paper was brought forward, DIAND organized the fishermen into co-operatives, and from that point on, despite a substantial investment by the department, production and the number of people employed by the fisheries both declined. Significantly, this happened at a time when Ministry of Natural Resources officials deny that the supply of fish was dwindling in any of the lakes being fished.

In retrospect, there were two reasons for the failure of the fisheries, both of which involved money and both of which DIAND failed to monitor. The most obvious was a substantial decline in the cash return on pickerel because of steady increases in the cost of flying the catch to market. This species was the bread and butter of the fisheries during the 1970s and usually accounted for approximately 60 per cent of their sales, but between 1970 and 1976 the net return to the fishermen plummeted from 87.5 cents to 54.0 cents per kilogram, and this resulted in a drop in average per capita earnings from $755 in 1970 to $457 in 1976. Unfortunately, instead of concentrating its investment in the fisheries in equalization payments to help the fishermen maintain their incomes, DIAND chose to spend its money on capital equipment such as docks, sheds, and ice-making machines.

Less obvious although no less important a problem was that, at the same time DIAND was trying to promote commercial fishing in the band, there was a massive increase in the number of make-work, job-training, and community-development programs that were being offered in the villages as a result of other White Paper initiatives. This meant that commercial fishing had to compete with programs such as BTSD, CMTP, OFY, LIP, and FLIP, and since these programs were more lucrative than fishing, the fishermen shifted their allegiance. In addition, commercial fishing was in competition with a tree-planting program sponsored by the Ministry of Natural Resources. Band members who went tree-planting could earn over $1,000 a month, but this usually happened in May, which was the time of year commercial fishermen had to prepare their equipment for the upcoming season. Given the difference in income, many fishermen chose to abandon fishing in favour of tree-planting. As more than one of them told us, the money in tree-planting was just too good.

Shuffle your feet

Work itself was not even used as an incentive to involve people in the band businesses. This was because when DIAND pursued job-creation as its goal, it often overstaffed the businesses to the point where work became so watered down and depreciated that it was almost a meaningless chore. For instance, although privately owned tourist camps in northern Ontario usually assign two guides to a party of four tourists, from 1969 to 1976 DIAND assigned four guides and one cook in the Webequie camp. Sometimes they were also accompanied by an assistant cook. Likewise, it was not unusual to find twice as many workers as were necessary to operate the sawmills. As one man from Fort Hope told us:

When Indian Affairs decided to build the sawmill up here, everyone knew there was no market for the lumber, except for what we needed for our own housing. The real reason they built the sawmill was to create jobs.

The way it worked was like this. Each year the people in the sawmill would produce only enough lumber for housing, but where you needed only two or three people to do the work, Indian Affairs made sure eight were hired.

This bizarre employment strategy placed employees under a tremendous strain. From their standpoint DIAND was forcing them to shuffle their feet. As one millworker in Fort Hope said: 'It wasn't that we didn't want to work hard, only that we couldn't, and that was one of the most frustrating things of all.' With little productive work to perform, the employees consequently took extra-long coffee breaks, showed up late in the morning, left early in the afternoon, and, as an ultimate humiliation, were often forced to pretend to be busy whenever some authority figure such as a business consultant or government official came around. In other words, work in the sawmills was reduced to the equivalent of putting in time, and the employees behaved accordingly, never being able to demonstrate the kind of effort that could have made the businesses a success.

Although counteracting forces prevented DIAND from overstaffing the fisheries, we also found evidence that work is no less important to fishermen than it is to millworkers and guides. In fact, one of the most dramatic demonstrations of the importance of work occurred in the fishery in Webequie in the summer of 1973. That summer, in order to increase the productivity of the fishery, DIAND sponsored a special fishing management and instruction program. However, at the beginning of the commercial fishing season in June, the fishermen discovered that the monthly income they would derive from the DIAND program would be less than they would receive if they went on welfare. After talking it over the fishermen decided to stop fishing. This situation prevailed until the DIAND official in charge of the program made an arrangement to have the fishermen paid the difference between their own fixed income and general assistance.[18] When the fishermen were told about this arrangement, fishing promptly resumed.

To the misfortune of both the band and the government, DIAND never heeded the lesson it was taught by the fishermen, and from 1969 through 1976 the department constantly manipulated band businesses so that genuine work opportunities were extremely rare. In retrospect, there can be little doubt that this was an enormous mistake.

Failing to recognize individual initiative

The last major flaw in DIAND's business-development strategy was that individual initiative was simply never recognized. In fact, some people were actually discouraged from starting their own businesses when all signs pointed to a definite commitment on their part. The tourist camps are a case in point.

In the summer of 1968, six men from Fort Hope built a log cabin to use as a tourist camp. This was done entirely on their own initiative and at their own expense. However, realizing that capital would be needed if they were going to compete with other tourist camps in the area, the partners approached DIAND for a loan. They were told that money was available, but only if the camp were owned by the band. In reality, ownership would rest with DIAND, but it was suggested that this was primarily for short-term protection and that, as soon as the camp was making a profit, the original partners would become the owners. To the partners this meant an obvious loss of control, but since they had no other source of financial support, they accepted DIAND's terms.

One of the partners explained how this happened:

We'd all worked as guides all over the place, but we were tired of working for others. We knew we could make money because everywhere around us camp operators were making money. So we built this cabin five miles from Fort Hope.

We all knew the tourists would like the camp because we built the cabin on a small peninsula with lots of trees and a beach at the point. The place always has a good breeze, so there aren't too many flies or mosquitoes either.

We only had one problem after it was finished. We needed boats, motors, and a little money to put ads in the newspapers. That was about it. But none of us had any money. That was the trouble, and that's why we went to Indian Affairs.

The man we talked to from Indian Affairs told us we would have no problem getting the money. That was when we first saw him. He said we had shown we meant business when we built the cabin and that a small loan could be arranged. That's what he said at the first meeting.

There were other meetings after, and at each one he told us different things. Finally, it ended like this: he would get us the money we were asking for, even more, and other camps would be built too, but only if the band owned the camps. Otherwise, he said, we would get nothing. So we went along with the plan because we had no other way of raising the money.

DIAND was true to its word. Within a short period of time five additional cabins were built near Fort Hope and a separate tourist camp was established for the people in Webequie, but since neither of the camps ever produced a profit, they remained under DIAND's control. As the man we just quoted explained:

I was put in charge of the Fort Hope camp because I spoke good English and knew a little about bookkeeping, but that never mattered much since the real decisions were made by Indian Affairs. They'd send a man up here every so often and he'd ask how things were going. Then he'd tell us what to do and how he wanted it done.

I'll give you an example. About three years ago Indian Affairs decided that since our bookings weren't too good, we should get a booking agent, someone from down south who had a phone, knew how to advertise, handle deposits, and all that. So Indian Affairs brought us all together, from Fort Hope and Webequie, and told us they had it all worked out. Our new booking agent was going to be a camp operator not far from here. But you know who he was? He was one of the biggest camp operators in the area, I'd say our biggest competitor. To have him handle our bookings would be taking a real chance because he could take the people who might come to our camps and send them to his.

We told this to Indian Affairs but they said there was no one else as good, and they could draw up a contract that would make sure he couldn't do anything to take away our customers. They said they'd put in a clause about a conflict of interest.

We still said we thought this was a bad idea and that everyone was against it. But you know what happened? They drew up that contract with the operator anyway, and they forced us to be with him for about two years. What we said didn't matter a damn, and a lot of bad feelings developed because of this.

Now that's just one decision that went against what we wanted. There were lots of others.

In other words, instead of supporting the people who might have established a successful tourist camp, DIAND created a situation in which the hopes of the original partners were destroyed. The price the partners paid to see the business get off the ground was a loss of ownership and control, and this was reflected in the way they performed. As their spokesman said:

Because the camp wasn't ours, it was never the same thing. It was Indian Affairs' camp, so we thought, why kill ourselves?

You know, if something's yours you care a lot more about it than if it isn't. So if Indian Affairs would have helped us like we asked at the beginning, things would have been a lot different than they are now. But they never gave us the chance we needed, and that's why we lost interest.

Requiem for a disaster

Finally, it is worthwhile pointing out that throughout the period when DIAND was introducing and managing band businesses, there was a general lack of consultation and accountability to the people in the band. The decisions to develop fisheries and sawmills and to modify the original plans for the co-op store and the tourist camps were taken by senior DIAND officials. Significantly, since job-creation was *the* issue of the day, aside from the feasibility study that was undertaken for the co-op store, no others were carried out to determine business potential or what scale of operation would be appropriate. As such, the success or failure of the businesses became DIAND's responsibility and not the responsibility of the band. If there were discussions with band members about the businesses, they were brief, at best token, and involved only day-to-day matters. But then, since there were no guidelines or operational plans for DIAND staff to follow, how could band members measure the department's performance or, for that matter, understand what their Indian agents were trying to achieve so that they could help?

In the end, the reaction to DIAND's manoeuvres ranged from sadness to disgust. A former chief put it to us this way:

When the first Indian Affairs economic-development adviser came up here to help us with the businesses – I think that was around 1969 or 1970 – he treated us in a very harsh way.

Looking back, I don't think that was so bad since he did get the businesses started. But what you have to remember is that he took away our pride. You see, it was always his ideas that were being developed and not ours, and this meant we never had any real input.

Over the years this has been one of our biggest problems with the businesses. Whatever Indian Affairs wants they get, so either we do it their way or we don't do it at all.

According to another:

If you look at the businesses carefully, you will see that all of them are the way they are because of the government. Every last one of them was set up by government, and every last one of them was interfered with by the government – the government being mainly Indian Affairs.

The end result is that the people see the businesses as only a small step up from welfare, and that's not much to say after all the time and money that was invested.

Moreover, since DIAND was also ready to subsidize business losses, albeit sometimes only after some arm-twisting, the inescapable conclusion from the people's point of view was that wastefulness was a practice that DIAND condoned. It was a process that one Indian Affairs report about Webequie described as follows:

The major problem confronting the Indian businesses in Webequie is the fact that they are all identified as being connected in some way with government. The 'concept' of 'government' is both foreign to the Ojibwa people and impossible to translate properly. Thus, most individuals see ... [the businesses] as being part of this thing 'government.' Government action in the community over the past ten years has fostered the idea that the government has lots of money to spend. Houses are built and given away; new motors appear for the camps after the older ones disappear; unemployment and welfare benefits are easily obtainable; and even the actions of Indian Affairs' staff, chartering planes, in one day and out the next, continue to support this belief of unlimited government money. Thus, there is now a dichotomy in the value and moral structure regarding personal property and government property. While the use of personal property binds the user to certain strict obligations, the use of government 'owned' materials is for everyone, but the responsibility of looking after or returning the equipment lies with no one. Therefore, for example, various individuals make use of the tourist camp equipment and abuse it, lose it, or steal it, knowing that it will be replaced, and that no action will be taken against them ... They do not see themselves as responsible for the successful operation of the businesses.

The same was unfortunately true in all the businesses DIAND tried to create in the band.

6

Freedom to fail

In January 1976 we reported most of what we have written about so far to a committee composed of two band officials and a group of middle-management government people, including two from DIAND, two from Manpower, and one each from the Ontario ministries of Natural Resources and Culture and Recreation.[1] Our report was based on socio-economic research we had conducted in the band communities during the previous year. The research was carried out under the auspices of LEAP – Manpower's Local Employment Assistance Program – and was undertaken, in part, to discover ways to help band businesses succeed.

In our report we said that in order to make effective plans for business development, the band's economy should be regarded as an evolving cultural system regulated by three main forces: community and family solidarity, income, and work. Seen in this way, significant events in the band's economic history formed a definite social pattern. For instance, when the schools were opened and band members shifted from trapping to welfare, solidarity and income were behind the move. Parents wanted to reunite their families and at the same time acquire enough money to satisfy their material needs. Later, when the people moved from welfare to White Paper initiatives, work and income were the reasons, and solidarity was maintained. And when DIAND's attempts to establish successful businesses failed, solidarity, income, and work once again were involved, except that this time, even though the businesses were located in the villages, or close enough that the people could visit their homes, low earnings and meaningless work made the businesses unattractive and ultimately unsuccessful. In other words, as long as the people had a stable social life, income and work seemed to be the two main factors that stimulated the band's economy to change.

The conclusion we reached was that for any band business to succeed, it would have to provide its employees with an adequate cash incentive – certainly more than they could acquire from welfare and White Paper programs – and a real chance to work. We also said that a business would stand an even greater chance of success if it were owned and operated by someone from the band rather than by the government. Our reasoning was that this not only would make it possible for the people to have local control but would allow employers to apply community standards to ensure that their employees were being paid enough money and provided with productive work. Finally, we said that with adequate refinancing and proper business-management assistance the failing DIAND businesses could probably be salvaged and made profitable. In particular, we felt this to be true for the tourist camps because of the strong potential market among sports fishermen in the midwestern United States.

Since our conclusions called into question the philosophy and reliability of existing policies and programs, we expected the government officials on the committee to react negatively to our report. They did not. They agreed with what we said. The consensus was that our analysis 'made sense' and offered a 'practical solution' to a pressing problem, not only in the Fort Hope Band but likely in many other bands. The officials also said that they were confident the people would soon reap the benefits.

To the band members who sat on the committee this was a clear signal that things were going to be different. One of them said: 'It's a good feeling to hear the government agree with what we've felt for a long time. I think now, for the first time, I can feel a bit of hope.'

In retrospect, all we were asking the committee to do was to give the band the resources to operate businesses and to let band members be the ones in control – really to give them the freedom to fail. But this was not to be. The committee was only an informal group with no real power to change the government's direction, and shortly after we had reported our findings, the committee dissolved, with each representative going his separate way and our conclusions forgotten.

The consequences for the band were considerable. What transpired after the committee dissolved was not what government officials on the committee supported and certainly not what band members wanted. Instead, between 1976 and 1980, LEAP officials, none of whom was on our committee, financed an ambitious and complicated project that involved five businesses organized under the umbrella of a large company called the Fort Hope Development Corporation. Four of the five businesses were tourist camps; the fifth was an inn with a restaurant. But because of convoluted LEAP regulations, individual ownership was prohibited, income was kept low, and all five businesses were tied to a complex funding formula that encouraged job-creation at the expense of meaningful work. In other words, the corporation was set up in a way that was completely antithetical to what we had suggested. Income, long-term employment opportunities, and control were all minimized, with predictably unfortunate results.

An overview of LEAP

By 1976 LEAP had been in existence for four years, and during that time it had gained the reputation of being the flagship of Manpower's programs. The arguments in its favour were impressive. Unlike other Manpower programs such as BTSD, CMTP, OFY, and LIP, LEAP did not provide funds to relieve short-term employment needs. Its mandate was to provide long-term funding to create permanent employment in economically depressed communities with chronically high unemployment, communities such as the ones in the Fort Hope Band. To fulfil this mandate, LEAP officials could provide projects with a great deal of money, up to $850,000 over a four-year period, with a maximum of $250,000 per year. LEAP could also be fairly flexible when it came to allowing groups to make business decisions on their own; unlike DIAND, Manpower was not interested in controlling the day-to-day operations of its projects. In addition, LEAP officials had the authority to become involved in an in-depth community consultation process, starting with a preliminary discussion of a proposed project with community representatives, perhaps leading to research such as we had done for the band. There was an opportunity for more consultation when a project submission was made to a LEAP regional review board, which included both government and community representatives. It was argued that, because of this long consultation process, LEAP was extremely sensitive to its clients' needs and LEAP officials could never be accused of acting unilaterally. The implication was that Manpower's LEAP program was far superior to anything DIAND had to offer.

But by the late 1970s there were strong indications that Manpower was having much the same problems with LEAP as DIAND was having with its business-development schemes. In a lengthy article titled 'Ottawa's Great LEAP Backward,' published in the November 1980 issue of *Canadian Business*, investigative reporter Ann Pappert said that after spending more than 200 million dollars, LEAP was by and large a failure and that only 3 per cent of its projects became viable businesses once LEAP funding ended.[2] The rest simply folded. Pappert also argued that LEAP policies doomed ventures to failure, that its staff was not trained properly, that controls over projects were poor, that funding often was terminated when projects were on the brink of success, that little flexibility was given to client groups, and that nothing was being done to see whether projects had succeeded in meeting their original objectives. She also said that 'Whether or not former LEAP employees ever do find jobs is a mystery, because no one follows them up to find out what happens to them. That is to say, the government hasn't the slightest idea what results it's got for its 200 million.'[3]

To be fair to LEAP, soon after the article appeared the minister of Employment and Immigration, Lloyd Axworthy, wrote a letter to *Canadian Business* in which he defended LEAP's record. Axworthy took strong exception to Pappert's claims, particularly the one that only 3 per cent of LEAP projects became viable businesses once funding had ended. He said that the figure was more like 62 per cent.[4] However, in a further letter to *Canadian Business* Pappert said that the minister's office had not provided her with any documentation of Axworthy's statistics and that in numerous talks with LEAP field staff she was told that 3 and sometimes 5 per cent were the actual figures.[5]

Important as it is, no matter whether the figure is 3, 5, or 62 per cent, the Pappert article identifies a number of problems with LEAP that not only compromise the chance for a project to succeed but bear a striking resemblance to the problems DIAND encountered in its business-development program. A good example of this is that by being first and foremost a job-creation program, LEAP concentrates on the number of jobs generated by a project at the expense of almost everything else. In fact, LEAP's formula for funding is not tied to business viability at all but to the number of jobs created – the more jobs, the more money LEAP is willing to provide. As such, sloppy business practices such as hiring too many employees are encouraged, whereas efficiency and viability are not. Also, relatively little money is available for capital purchases, and this makes business ventures that require large initial capital outlays difficult to finance, a serious problem in native communities where problems of capital formation are critical and the only recourse is to approach still other government agencies for funding, perhaps ultimately tying a project to two, three, or four separate agencies. As a consequence, LEAP policies encourage complex and difficult financing arrangements that handicap projects from the start. The experience of the Fort Hope Development Corporation with LEAP certainly supports this view.

The Fort Hope Development Corporation

Shortly after the committee that we had reported to dissolved, LEAP officials instructed the band to draft a proposal to present to a LEAP regional review board. The proposal, they said, should follow the lines of our research recommendations and focus on a take-over and redevelopment of the two failing DIAND tourist camps by individuals in the band. However, in subsequent meetings with more senior LEAP officials there was a striking turn-about in Manpower's position. The senior officials said point-blank that the only way their program could be used to fund a business in the band was if the business were either non-profit or band-owned. Individual ownership, they argued, was 'not democratic' since it favoured the owners and left Manpower and LEAP open to a charge of playing favourites. They also said that since LEAP was aimed at job-creation, the amount the band hoped to get to start a project would depend on the number of jobs created. As for capital purchases, crucial to developing the tourist camps and the inn, the funds for those businesses would have to come from other government agencies.

This was a severe blow to the band representatives who served on our committee, since they had been led to believe that LEAP was more flexible than DIAND. But even when they argued vehemently against organizing a business in this way and pointed out that senior LEAP officials were ignoring the research on which the project was supposed to be based, they were told bluntly that no other options were available. LEAP policy would not allow it. One senior LEAP official put it this way: 'If the band wants LEAP money, if they want to have jobs, and if they want a new business, then they're just going to have to fit themselves into our way of doing things or they'll get nothing.' The band representatives were also told that if they were going to submit a proposal, they had better do so as soon as possible; otherwise there was no guarantee that funds would be available for the project the band wanted to develop. There were other bands with other proposals to be considered. The Fort Hope Band was only one among many.

These rules placed the band in an extremely difficult position. They could either insist on individual ownership and lose out on LEAP funding or give in on the ownership issue and forget about an important incentive that very likely would help the tourist camps succeed. Also, since job-creation was to be emphasized and relatively little money made available for capital equipment, efficiency and possibly viability might have to be sacrificed. In other words, the price of LEAP funding was high.

But with high unemployment and poverty a fact of life in the villages, the band's response was painfully predictable. LEAP offered jobs and a chance to earn a living, and it was hard to refuse, even if that meant going against what the band believed was right. After discussing the problem, band members decided to concede to LEAP and participate in the program. As the person who became the president of the Fort Hope Development Corporation told us later: 'There we were after all that research work, everyone promising to change things, and still we were going to get the run-around. But we had no choice. Unemployment was high, and we needed what LEAP was offering. They called the shots, and we had to go along.'

The proposal

In the fall of 1976 the band submitted its proposal to the LEAP regional review board. From the point of view of the band the submission was a compromise and, under the circumstances, certainly an optimistic state-ment about what it hoped to accomplish. First, the band wanted to create three tourist-camp businesses by taking over the two failing DIAND camps and a third one DIAND had built for the people in Ogoki, around seventy-five kilometres from Fort Hope. Later, a fourth camp near Lansdowne was added. The proposal said that DIAND was willing to transfer the camps if LEAP funding were obtained. Since there was a strong American market to the south, it was argued that finding customers would not be a problem. All that was required was adequate promotion to get tourists interested, reasonable prices to encourage them to come, streamlined service for repeat business, and good fishing, which the proposal said was guaranteed. Some work also had to be done to refurbish the old DIAND cabins, which had fallen into a state of disrepair, and to build a few others at attractive locations.

Second, the band wanted to open an inn-restaurant in Fort Hope. To do this the band wanted to use LEAP funds to purchase the co-op manager's residence, which had been built alongside the store but was now standing empty. In the meantime DIAND officials had let it be known that the department was prepared to turn the large house over to the band for a nominal sum if LEAP would provide the funds for renovations. Once again it was suggested that customer demand would not be a problem. Gov-ernment officials were visiting Fort Hope with greater frequency than ever before, and DIAND had agreed to close its 'Indian Affairs cabin,' where government officials usually stayed, as soon as the inn opened.

This would give the inn a monopoly, and if that was not enough, there was a strong likelihood that many more tourists would be arriving on their way to the camps.

Third, as far as ownership and management were concerned, the band agreed that for the time being it would go along with LEAP requirements and avoid individual ownership, as long as later on, when LEAP funding was no longer required, the band would be allowed to partition the corporation into five separate businesses that individual band members could own and operate as they saw fit. The people most likely to take over the businesses would be the ones who had managed them while they were being supported by LEAP.

Finally, the band agreed to have the corporation set up as a non-profit enterprise and requested funds to hire a full-time management consultant to train the people who would be running the camps and the inn-restaurant. The band also said that it wanted the co-ordination of tourist-camp bookings to be the responsibility of a band member who would be stationed at the central office in Fort Hope. The booking agent would also act as the corporation's president.

Given what appeared to be a workable plan, the LEAP regional review board approved the band's submission unanimously, and from 1977 until funding was terminated four years later, Manpower invested a total of $800,000 in the corporation. The results of this massive investment were at first glance impressive. Over the life of LEAP's involvement, the corporation produced over $700,000 in revenue and generated more than 2,000 man-weeks of work. But these achievements were accomplished in spite of LEAP and not because of it. Throughout the corporation's history LEAP policies minimized the incentives that might have made it succeed. Control, money, and work were all parcelled out in small amounts; by the summer of 1981 only two of the five businesses had made any profits, and together the most profit those two businesses made in a single year was only $11,000. As for the future, unless new sources of funding are found, the corporation may very well go bankrupt.

Control

Perhaps the most serious problem the corporation encountered arose when the band tried to solve the problem of individual ownership and control. In the end this issue almost tore the corporation apart.

Since LEAP insisted that the corporation had to be owned by the band, the chief and council selected eight people to manage the businesses and serve as the corporation's board of directors.[6] These men were chosen because they had put considerable time and energy into developing the original DIAND tourist camps and because they already had experience. The band's plan was for them to become the owners of the businesses but, in the meantime, to have them operate the businesses independently, as if they were their own. Only for LEAP 'paperwork' would the businesses be considered parts of a larger, single corporate entity.

Moreover, LEAP officials agreed to let the board handle all the major decisions and set corporate policy, on the understanding that if the corporation did produce a profit, it could either be reinvested or be distributed among the eight as a cash bonus at the end of each fiscal year. Then, at the end of four years, when LEAP funding was terminated, the eight could buy out of the parent corporation for a nominal sum and establish their own businesses. In this way eight people were told that if they would only be patient, they would become the owners of their own businesses.

The trouble with these arrangements was that when it came time to have them formalized, it was discovered that they were illegal. As managers of a non-profit corporation the board could not be employed by the corporation simultaneously, since this created a conflict of interest. In view of this problem, the lawyer advising the corporation suggested that the eight continue as managers but resign as directors and have themselves replaced by a 'safe' board, hopefully including their friends and relatives. The lawyer also suggested that the new board have no more than three directors, that the directors only meet once a year, and that at their annual meeting all corporate decisions be ratified without question. To expedite matters further he suggested that only one director would have to be present to hold an official meeting. In other words, a dummy corporation would be set up. But as the lawyer who made these suggestions admitted: 'Even for people who know a lot about corporations, this is complex.'

Although the paperwork covering these manoeuvres was completed almost immediately, it was impossible to install a safe board in office since the corporation's existing board could not agree on who should be selected, so the managers continued to serve on the board. Unfortunately, due to the vast distances between the businesses, a lack of adequate telephone service, and a LEAP policy that initially required the managers to contact each other before they spent any money, the corporation was soon bogged down in red tape. By the end of the first year only one of the businesses had made any profit, and none of the managers was pleased with the way things were going.

In the meantime, the job of running the day-to-day operations of the corporation was increasingly assumed by its president, and this eventually led to a good deal of misunderstanding between the individual managers. There were two reasons for this. First, since all records, correspondence, bank deposits, pay-roll information, and customer bookings were handled by the central office, none of the managers was able to grasp the operation of the corporation as a whole – only the president could. Second, LEAP accountants often wanted to know what the corporation's cash flow was going to be at a given point in the year so they could release cheques on time, and this meant drawing up budgets for each business and forecasting its total revenue and expenditures. But since it was often impossible to bring everyone together because of costs, prior commitments, and bad weather, and since only the president had all the information, he was usually forced to do the planning himself.

The result was that the managers outside of Fort Hope felt that they were having their businesses run for them much as DIAND had done before. The situation became so bad that by 1979 the managers of the Webequie tourist camp pulled out of the corporation, choosing to forgo LEAP funding entirely rather than have no control. An excerpt from a letter written by them to the president just before they left leaves no doubt about their reasons for withdrawing:

To tell you the truth, we the Webequie Camp owners, feel uneasy that we will never learn to run our own camps if someone is always doing it for us. Since we have been with the camps from the start we feel less interested as the years go by because we cannot run our own camps.

We are now asking if we can leave or get out of the Fort Hope Development Corporation this year. We wish to be on our own.

We the Webequie River Camp owners, will never learn if we never try to run our own camps. We are now in the same situation as when we started off. Our camps are always run by somebody.

This was a very painful experience for the president. He felt that he had been carrying the corporation himself, working to make all of the businesses succeed, yet the managers outside of Fort Hope were not satisfied. As he told us:

When I look at the corporation and the people who are the managers, the ones who are supposed to be the eventual owners, all I see is a group of people who are confused and disappointed and not really running the businesses the way they thought they would.

Because the corporation is funded by LEAP, it has one bank account and one set of books – those are LEAP requirements – and one central office that takes care of everything from bookings to purchasing. This means there is only one person who knows what's happening, and that's me.

As for the other managers, since they're located in different communities with no books, no bank accounts, no way to see bills, and no way to accept bookings, well, it's just impossible for them to participate.

So it's my opinion the people are confused and disappointed because they got something they never really expected. They thought they would be able to manage the businesses on their own, but that has been impossible since none of the businesses are funded on their own. That would have been the best way to do it, and it should have been done from the start.

Income

Perhaps the managers would have been less disappointed if they had been allowed to share in the profits, as they were led to believe they would be. Although it was true that LEAP officials had first agreed to allow the corporation either to reinvest profits or to distribute them as a bonus, when it came down to actual implementation, paying out a bonus was considered frivolous, and only reinvestment was allowed. Only in one instance was this rule broken, when $500 was paid out to each of the managers, and this was done because the president was determined to show them that extra cash would be forthcoming if everyone worked to make a profit. At the time, he was attempting to relate business perform-ance to effort, but under LEAP policies further payments of this sort were vetoed, despite the fact that profits were relatively small and most of the time the businesses lost money. As the president explained: 'All we had were salaries and that was it. Each manager got $200 a week, and this was later increased to $250. But what I wanted to do was to show them they could get more if they made a profit. That was what we were in there for, you know. But with LEAP it was no! Anyway, I got to do it once, and for a short time it really picked up everyone's feelings.'

There were other ways in which income was controlled. By weighting its funding towards wages and excluding large capital purchases, LEAP prevented the corporation from buying a small Beaver airplane that might have allowed it to run a more profitable and efficient operation. As it was, the corporation was forced to lease planes whenever it had to fly tourists into its camps, and this ate up most of its revenue. It also made the corporation dependent on outside airline companies, and since a number of them ran their own tourist camps, Fort Hope customers did not always get the best service. However, the corporation could do little about this problem, not even fund a feasibility study to determine the cost-effectiveness of purchasing a plane, since this was also vetoed by LEAP.

Meanwhile, in the corporation's second year of operation it paid out $79,178 for air transportation, while total camp revenues were only $146,526. Based on an estimated price of $90,000 for a reconditioned Beaver – equivalent to what the airlines in the area were using – the corporation likely would have been able to justify the purchase, all the more so if other band enterprises such as servicing trappers on their traplines and making small freight hauls between the villages had been taken into account.

As for other sources of funds that could have helped the corporation purchase the plane or make other investments, here too the people were stymied, mainly because LEAP regulations made the corporation a non-profit enterprise. There are two good examples of this. First, when the corporation approached DIAND's Indian Economic Development Fund for financial assistance, it was told that funding non-profit businesses was out of the question since this went against the very essence of what business was all about, namely, making money. Then, when the corporation approached the province of Ontario and the Department of Regional Economic Expansion under their Joint Special Agricultural and Resource Development Agreement – at the urging of federal and provincial officials – they were told that they were ineligible for funding because the corporation was not publicly owned.

Work

Finally, because of LEAP policies that encouraged hiring more people than were really necessary, even work was often devalued in the corporation. A good example of this occurred in the Webequie tourist camp, which continued to hire too many guides even when both the corporation's president and outside consultants recommended against doing so. But since LEAP paid wages regardless of business efficiency, there was no real reason for the Webequie managers not to overstaff and, with high unemployment in the community, every reason to continue the practice. This fact was mentioned in a LEAP-sponsored evaluation of the corporation undertaken in 1979 by two independent consultants from Lakehead University's School of Business:

It apears that consideration should be given to assessing fulltime staffing commitments in the clerical section of the operation as well as in the use of dock and maintenance staff. The consultant's question, as a result of witnessing several hours of idle time being put in by employees in these two areas, is whether or not some overstaffing has occurred.[7]

The LEAP evaluators also had this to say:

With respect to the objective of creating employment in a chronically high unemployment area, the project has met with reasonable success in that approximately 1800 man-weeks of work have been provided by the project to date. However, the results here must be tempered somewhat since questions must be raised about the actual need for this amount of labour ... [and] the impact such a level of employment has on the profitability of the Corporation.[8]

Also, one has to wonder what impact overstaffing had on the people who had no productive work to do. Did they learn anything besides poor work habits? Did they feel good about their jobs? Likely they did not, although it would not be correct to leave the impression that working for the corporation was equivalent to working in the DIAND businesses. There was never any rampant shuffling of feet; the corporation's president and the managers worked hard to ensure that this did not happen. Nevertheless, since there was the LEAP funding formula to contend with and high unemployment, the tendency to overstaff was irresistible.

A dim future

Although the corporation managed to have two of its tourist camps generate operating profits in 1980, the future does not look bright for any of the five businesses, and this is especially true for the four tourist camps. At the present time the camps have a monopoly on using the lakes and rivers in the area for tourism because the Ministry of Natural Resources discriminates in their favour. But the ministry may change this practice as the demand for access to the far north increases and as political pressure is applied by southern operators – ministry officials already have said as much to the band council. Once this happens, the tourist camps, without a plane of their own to enhance profits, something their competitors already have, will find it even more difficult to make a profit.

Still, the people in the corporation have one thing going for them. In

1980 LEAP funding was terminated according to the terms of the original agreement, and this has left the managers free to hire workers as the business needs of the corporation dictate. The people in the corporation also know that when they do make a profit, they can do with it what they like. Nor is there any longer an involved corporate structure to contend with. But where will they go for the working capital they are surely going to need, for boats and motors, advertising, promotion, and so on, especially since only two of the camps are in the black? Will they go to the banks? That is unlikely, since the banks have up to now been reluctant to lend money to band businesses because the people do not have enough collateral and Indian businesses are generally regarded as poor risks. No doubt these factors would weigh heavily in the minds of bank officials if they heard that after four years of LEAP funding, worth almost one million dollars, only two of the corporation's businesses ever made a profit. Likely the businesses will disappear. In 1982 DIAND said that it would grant the corporation $350,000 – $50,000 a year for seven years – if the managers wanted to continue. They refused.

Distant dreams

One evening in the spring of 1979, one of us was sitting at a table in a small two-room office in Fort Hope with six of the corporation's directors. They were talking about the corporation, each one taking his turn, and they were in a sombre mood. The Webequie people were pulling out. Only one business, the Fort Hope camp, was making a profit. DIAND was taking its time to transfer the camps to the corporation – no one knew if that really was going to happen – and LEAP was sending in two consultants to evaluate the corporation for its fourth year of funding. LEAP was concerned that the corporation had not yet made significant profits.

The president spoke at length. He said that although things were going badly, they had no choice but to stay with LEAP. No one else would give them a dime, and if they decided to forget about LEAP, who would loan them money?

Then a second person spoke up and said that he agreed it was best to stay with LEAP. A third followed and a fourth, each offering his views. No one was happy with LEAP, but there was no place else to turn.

The conversation went on late into the night until, after reaching no conclusion, everyone turned to what they had hoped for and what they had dreamed. The president spoke most eloquently of all, and his words are well worth quoting. They summarize in many ways the frustrations and dreams of many of the Fort Hope people:

All I ever wanted for myself and my family was a small tourist camp that I could make a living out of. That's all I wanted. And I know that's all everybody around this room wanted.

And I suppose, too, that's all a lot of Indian people ever want – a chance to make something for themselves without always having to go to the government for help. But our dreams are always just dreams because of the government, and I think they always will be just dreams.

We ask them for help and they always say: 'Yes, we'll help you,' but they never tell you about all the strings attached. You can have money for your business but don't make money. You can have money for your business but don't try too much to compete because we won't let you. You can have money for your business but make sure you run a job-creation program at the same time.

And then they ask: 'Why doesn't your business run on its own? Why do you always need government money?' And they ask you this without knowing they are the ones who are responsible. They just seem to forget.

Maybe some day things will change. I hope so, because if they don't, my sons and your sons will go from here, and you and I will want them to.

7

From Lansdowne House to Summer Beaver

One late afternoon in the summer of 1975, when we first saw Lansdowne House from the air, we looked down on what appeared to be an ideal place – a small village spread out over two islands tucked away on a lake in the wilderness, a few houses, a school, a church, the sun setting on the horizon. It seemed to be a truly beautiful place, with a certain gentle, almost timeless quality to it. But when our float-plane landed and we were standing on the dock, Lansdowne House was very different indeed. In the distance, from inside one of the houses, we heard someone crying and then yelling; not far from us, in front of the community hall, two young men were drunk; and everywhere else we looked there were run-down buildings covered in graffiti, scattered oil drums, rusting snow-machines, and garbage. It was hard to believe that what we had seen from the air was as truly miserable as what we now faced. But a walk through the village only confirmed our worst thoughts – more run-down buildings, more graffiti, more discarded oil drums, more rusting snow-machines, a sewer system started but never completed, and garbage as far as the eye could see. We also passed a group of young men and women who were drinking openly and laughing loudly. One of the men screamed at us; another laughed; a bottle was held up for us to see; then it was smashed. The group looked at us for a moment, undecided about encircling us, and then turned back, indifferent to who we were and what we were doing in Lansdowne. There was in the scene in front of us and indeed in all of Lansdowne nothing gentle or timeless or beautiful, only tension and a potential for violence that was all too real.

Our initial impression of Lansdowne was not the only surprise that the community held in store for us. As we were still getting to know the people there, we witnessed a strange event that shocked and confused us at the time. In the summer of 1975, ninety people moved from Lansdowne House to a new community they called 'Nibinamic' – Summer Beaver. They were all Anglican; only Catholics remained in Lansdowne. The government did not precipitate the move. Trouble had been brewing in the community for years, although most of the time it had been kept under control. But by the summer of 1975 Lansdowne House was a place where drinking, vandalism, and violence dominated the residents' lives.

Examples were numerous. Two days after we arrived, we talked to an officer from the Ontario Provincial Police who visited the community on a regular basis. He told us that there was no other place like Lansdowne: 'The community is something out of the Dark Ages ... drinking days on end ... trying to kill each other ... young girls, kids really, raped ... nothing and no one is safe.'

He told us that the pattern of drinking and violence was always the same and always started when someone either brought liquor in from a trip down south or chartered a plane to fly it in. And it was difficult to do anything about the bootlegging because it was not illegal to bring liquor into the village. Lansdowne is not inside a reserve and, under the Indian Act, this makes it impossible for the local council to pass a by-law making possession of liquor an offence. All the police could do was wait until trouble broke out, fly in, and make arrests. The officer gave us no explanation as to why the village was so troubled, only that young men were the worst offenders.

The young men did not deny the charge. They had come to regard drinking and violence as a way of life. One of them told us this story as if it were nothing out of the ordinary:

When I'm here I drink every opportunity I can, and after I'm drunk I can't seem to stay out of trouble. A little while ago I ended up in jail because I got into a fight with this guy I was drinking with. It happened like this: This guy and me got pretty loaded, and then we decided to go to the adult-education building where some of the people were playing pool. When we got there I told him not to disturb anyone, but he got mad and started to push me around. That made me mad, so I dragged him outside and we wrestled on the ground. We fought for a few minutes with me winning, and then I let him go. When he got up he told me I'd be sorry.

Later that night I heard that my house had been torn apart – a brand new house – and that my wife and kids had to run. I went to look for myself, and I saw that everything was broken. All the windows were smashed and everything else was ruined – furniture, dishes, everything. I found out it was the same guy I was fighting with earlier. He'd been with two other guys and they'd threatened my wife.

So I went after this guy, and when I caught up with him at my sister's house I took him outside and beat him up. When he begged me not to hit him anymore I stopped, but I was charged with assault and sentenced to eight days in jail. Since then I've been in other fights, but that's the way it is up here. Either you fight or you don't survive.

Another young man told us that one of his friends had gone berserk and tried to kill the Catholic priest in Lansdowne. During Sunday mass he walked into church with a rifle and aimed it at the priest. Fortunately, someone grabbed the rifle, and the frightened parishioners wrestled the man to the floor before he could shoot.

It was clear that Lansdowne was being torn apart, and this was confirmed in August 1975 when the Anglicans packed their belongings and moved to Summer Beaver, where peace and quiet were restored. Meanwhile, in Lansdowne, the drinking and violence continued.

During the years that followed the move we often wondered why Lansdowne alone was so troubled and not the other band communities. The story we were able to piece together is strange and frightening, strange because it involves a prophecy that the world would end, which many people believed, and frightening because it shows how vulnerable the band villages really are to government cut-backs and how much they depend on the government for support. Without this support Summer Beaver likely would have collapsed, whereas in Lansdowne cut-backs are threatening the community's life. Once again, in order to protect the anonymity of our sources, we will not provide specific references for internal government reports.

The origin of discontent

The trouble in Lansdowne dates back to the early 1960s, when the community was formed. The people who came there arrived in small, closely knit kinship groups from different locations and with different religious views, Anglicans moving in from the north and west and Catholics from the south.[1] The upshot of these differences was that the people were uncomfortable with each other from the start, and when they came together, they immediately divided themselves into two distinct groups, factions really, which looked to different leaders. First there were the Anglicans, who turned to one of their own people for guidance, and then there were the Catholics, who were led by an Oblate priest.

The Catholics did not select the priest by accident. By the early 1960s he had been a missionary among them for more than a decade, was fluent in Ojibwa, and was always quick to take an active interest in the day-to-day affairs of his congregation. Among other things he acted as a liaison between the community and government, encouraged DIAND to provide educational facilities and materials for the people, and promoted the use of snowmachines in the band. In addition, the priest was instrumental in helping the Catholics to organize a food co-op, start a sawmill, and market the handicrafts they produced. The priest fell easily into the role of a leader.

But from the Anglicans' standpoint the priest was a dangerous man. Their first missionaries had told them that Catholics were evil. As the priest told us: 'The trouble between the Anglicans and myself goes back to the missionaries who converted the people. Anglicans were told to stay away from Catholics and Catholics were told to stay away from Anglicans, and this problem has never been resolved.' We were also told that when Lansdowne was originally formed, it was common practice for Anglican missionaries to preach strong sermons not only against Catholic dogma but against the priest who lived among them.

Whether by accident or design, the two churches also dealt with their congregations in different ways, especially in terms of the amount of time they spent in the village. For instance, instead of settling in Lansdowne as the Catholic priest had done, Anglican missionaries visited the settlement intermittently. The Anglicans told us that this was done to encourage them to select their own leaders, which they did, and they maintained the tradition of regarding the priest with suspicion.

If the government was aware of the political and religious strife that existed in the community, it likely thought it unimportant, and during the 1970s federal and provincial agencies proceeded to make the same programs available in Lansdowne that they were offering in Fort Hope and Webequie, with the same results. In retrospect, this is hard to understand because, at the same time that government involvement was increasing, there was a dramatic increase in drinking and violence in the settlement, particularly among young Catholic men in their teens and early twenties.

Week-ends often started with a break-in at the fuel shed, where the young men could find gasoline to sniff, or with a homebrew drinking party, or, if they had the money, with liquor they chartered in from the south. Once they were high, they would stagger around, pick fights, and vandalize. When this happened, the police were asked to fly in to restore order, and at times this meant that people were tied to trees. Still, nothing seemed to work, and from 1969 to 1975 members of the Catholic gang were charged with theft, rape, and attempted murder.

Even the Catholic church was not beyond attack. Money and communion wine were stolen, windows were smashed, and the priest's life was threatened for a second time when a young woman barged into the rectory and attacked him while he was eating his evening meal. The priest was shaken by these events, driven to the point where he was forced to admit that he could no longer communicate with the younger members of his congregation. He explained it to us this way:

None of our young people go beyond grade twelve. They send them to
Geraldton for high school, and none of them succeed. Then they come back
here, and the trouble starts.

They know too much to trap and not enough to have a trade, so they have
nothing to do except wait until they have enough money to buy liquor and
get drunk.

We had a man from Alcoholics Anonymous come up here to talk to the
young people. He told them how he had been an alcoholic before, how liquor
is terrible, how it ruins your life, destroys your family, and how everything
gets worse until you finally kill yourself.

Nothing he said impressed them, and frankly, I don't know what can be
done to make them listen.

However, the priest could not explain why the other young men in the band were not as troubled as those in Lansdowne, including those in Fort Hope and Webequie who also went out to school.

Perhaps it was the priest who, being non-Indian, older, and a man of the cloth, was simply unable to bridge the cultural and generational gap between himself and the young Catholics. If the differences had not been so great – say, for instance, he had been chosen from within their own ranks – perhaps then he could have been an effective leader for all the Catholics and not just the old. He even admitted to us that he wondered about his overall impact on the community and if it had been for the good. Sadly, he said to us once about the young Catholics: 'I baptized them, confirmed them, heard their confessions, and watched them grow up, but I no longer know them.' In any event, the problems in the Catholic population were complex and deeply rooted, and in Lansdowne House, unlike the other band villages, community solidarity was impossible to maintain.

Prelude to the end

By 1972 the number of violent episodes in Lansdowne had reached a disturbing level, and this was particularly upsetting to the Anglicans, who were often the target of Catholic attacks. They were now living among totally unpredictable people, and as their community disintegrated around them, they sent word to DIAND through an intermediary that a group of sixty Anglicans intended to leave Lansdowne and return to their ancestral home at Nibinamic Lake. The intermediary called the Anglicans 'the people of Summer Beaver' and explained their plan in a letter he wrote to DIAND's district office in December 1972:

Dear Sir:
The people of Summer Beaver have asked me to write this letter to you and tell you that they have chosen Summer Beaver as their reserve.

There are approximately 60 people ... [who want to move], but when others come from Webequie and Wunnummin [Lake Reserve] there will be about 250 ...

The people who asked me to write you ... [would like to] have an answer from you in the near future as there will be a meeting in January.

If you require any additional information I will try and get it.

I am yours sincerely ...

The district office responded by sending an Indian agent to Lansdowne to interview the Anglicans and prepare a background report on who intended to move, why they considered the move important, and how they planned to support themselves in the new community. The report was completed eight months later, and in it the author noted: 'It is significant that, without exception, those families now proposing to move are all members of the original 'Summer Beaver' class. For various reasons already discussed [including religious differences, drinking, and violence], it appears that they are trying to recreate as far as possible the former (presumably happier) extended family relationships which they previously enjoyed.' He also said that the people making the move were planning to ask the federal government to provide them with schools, housing, assistance with economic development, and health services.

DIAND discussed the report with other government agencies, and they all agreed to withhold their support. They were afraid that the costs might be astronomical if the government adopted a policy of funding unplanned breakaway communities. When word filtered back to the Anglicans, they decided to postpone the move since they knew there was no way they could support themselves without government help. However, less than twelve months later the Anglicans became involved in a deeply religious and terrifying experience that not only caused them to redouble their efforts to get to Summer Beaver but gave government officials good reason to rethink their original position.

The end of the world

The event that set things in motion occurred on 10 October 1973. It was on that day, while he was trapping near a stream, that an Anglican named Stephen[2] had a vision in which God told him that the world would be destroyed within a matter of months. Stephen's vision had a profound impact on his Anglican neighbours. Formerly a quiet man, Stephen was miraculously transformed into an orator, so effective, in fact, that he was able to convince the Anglican leaders that his vision was real. The leaders in turn convinced most of the other Anglicans that Stephen was right, and for the next six months, until Easter, the time picked for the end, none of them worked and none of them sent their children to school. Each day was a ritual of church meetings, prayer, and fasting.[3]

At first, even the Catholics were convinced that the world was going to end. If not for the priest they also might have stopped working and sending their children to school. But the priest told them to wait, and so they waited impatiently until January 1974, when Stephen and the priest had a show-down. Stephen never spoke to us about the confrontation; the priest did:

In January, three months after Stephen's vision, a lot of my people were starting to go and hear what Stephen was saying. But by then it was not just Stephen who was saying that the end was coming. There were two other Anglican leaders who were saying the same thing, and they were all very convincing.

You can believe me that by then it was a very powerful experience. Every-one was in church, from morning to night, praying to God for forgiveness and preparing themselves for the final judgment. The children did not go to school; they were in church too. Those who were sick wouldn't go to the nurse; they thought there was no need. Even eating was restricted, almost to the point where the co-op and the Bay had to close.

It was a very serious thing, and my people were excited and starting to believe, because by then God was not only speaking to Stephen but to the Anglican leaders too. They thought they were truly enlightened. They were seeing all sorts of visions and thought they were not here on this earth.

I knew I had to do something, so I went over to see Stephen – this was the 10th of January – and I asked him if we could meet with the community as a whole. I said to Stephen: 'There are Catholics who have been hearing you talk for a long time now, and we would like to know when we are going to die and how. Would you like to come to the parish hall and speak, explain to us when you received your vision, and everything else that's happened to this day?'

Stephen said: 'Okay! We'll start this morning, right at eleven.'

The settlement chairman quickly went around to tell everyone about the meeting, and at exactly eleven, the meeting started. It lasted for seven hours, without one break, and everyone in the community was there, all the whites too.

The meeting was one long talk after another, with Stephen and the two Anglican leaders taking turns telling everyone about their visions. They got better as they went along, and while they were talking they quoted one passage from the Bible after another.

For instance, their vision of the end went right along with the Crucifixion and the Resurrection. We were all supposed to die on Good Friday. On Easter Sunday we would be resurrected to face the Final Judgment, and forty days later the faithful would ascend to heaven.

They also told about their visions of Judgment, Heaven, and Hell, and what it would all be like, again taking a lot from the Bible. It was all very powerful because the Bible gave them authority, but I knew what to do and I was ready.

Towards the end of the meeting I stood up and said: 'I believe everything you've said, even a little more, but there's one thing missing, one thing to make what you've said complete.'

I took my Bible in my hands. I told them that what they were saying was true because it was in the Bible, and that the Bible was the word of God. But I also said that we had to talk about everything that was in the Bible, not just one part. I went on to quote Matthew 24:36, where God tells us about the end: 'But of that day and hour knoweth no man, no, not the angels of heaven, but my Father only.'

Then I said: 'Now, you're telling us that you know the date when the end is going to happen because God told you. But how can that be, since the Bible says that no one will know the date, not even the angels? So how can you say that you know?'

Stephen answered: 'I've been enlightened! I've been chosen! You haven't!'

I couldn't answer that, so I said: 'I don't know the date of the end. I haven't been chosen. God didn't tell me because he said he wouldn't tell anyone. So there's only one thing I have to say to you. Either God's crazy or you're crazy, and I don't think it's God that's crazy. I have no more to say.'

The Catholics in the hall all yelled out that I was right, but the Anglicans said nothing. There was no shaking them.

Under the circumstances, even the older Catholics were forced to admit that the Anglicans were wrong, and when this happened, the rift in the community widened. The Anglicans became the butt of crude jokes and a vile stream of ridicule and scorn, and when the end never came, Stephen and the Anglican leaders retreated to the bush while their believers remained in Lansdowne, very much shaken and disheartened. Finally, they could take it no longer, and in August 1975 a group of eighty-three Anglicans, including Stephen and the leaders, left Lansdowne, migrated to Summer Beaver, and began to build houses.

Summer Beaver is established

The people who moved to Summer Beaver were a homogeneous group. Not only were they all Anglican; most were related to each other through traditional patrilineal ties. Moreover, almost all of them had either lived in Summer Beaver before or were the descendants of people who had moved to Lansdowne from Summer Beaver in the past.

In the beginning, reports about the new community were encouraging. An Indian agent who visited the people in August 1975 wrote:

The effort being put into the new community is prodigious, and the results are so far a tribute to the determination and ingenuity of the individuals concerned. Although the community has no real economic base at this point, neither have any other communities in the area of Ontario north of the CNR. Because the population is based strictly on kinship, on the other hand, the new community could be more socially stable than most, and could become a viable unit for that reason alone.

A representative from the Indian Community Secretariat reached the same conclusion when he paid the people a visit five months later. He found the place a beehive of activity:

As of January 1976, 30 buildings had been erected. They are all of log construction and consist of: 25 homes, a church, a band office, a workshop, a small store and a small warehouse.

A dock has also been constructed to enable aircraft to easily unload supplies.

All buildings have been laid out as if surveyed. The community has been thoughtfully planned; it is suitable for future services.

A daily newspaper in the south even put in a good word for Summer Beaver. In a story published shortly after the community was established, the people were described as 'a hardy group of pioneering Native people, seeking a link with the land and good life of their ancestors.'[4]

But the people were not only seeking a link with the land. While they were completely committed to the move for obvious reasons, they realized that they could not abandon the economic support the government had provided them with in Lansdowne. This was made abundantly clear in a question-and-answer session the residents had with the DIAND official who visited them in the summer of 1975, when the community was only one month old. As he noted in his report:

I asked the Summer Beaver group a number of questions. Their answers were well prepared.

Q: I can see that there are a large number of people at Summer Beaver. How many will return to Lansdowne for the winter?
A: None.
Q: If you are going to stay at Summer Beaver, will you send your children to Lansdowne to attend school?
A: No. All the children will stay here, but we hope to have a school, and will build it ourselves if necessary. We already asked ... for a teacher, and know one ... who would be willing to come.
Q: How do you hope to make your living at Summer Beaver?
A: The fish and game are more plentiful here, and we believe that we can obtain many of our daily needs from the land. We will, of course, need some cash since we have to buy some things from the store. Some will come from trapping and fishing, some from government assistance.

Q: You mentioned government assistance for your cash needs. Do you plan to ask the government for anything else?
A: Of course. We need some things now, and others for the future.
Q: What are the most important things which you think the government can supply?

[At this point a list was developed that included social assistance, mail and freight service, medical facilities, a school, radio communications, a store, and community development.]

Holding steadfastly to their position, the residents repeated their demands to the Indian Community Secretariat agent who visited them in December. The message in his report was just as clear:

The representatives of Summer Beaver have made it clear that they have no intention of 'going it alone.' Their return has been misinterpreted by some as a return to the land; I do not think there ever was such an intention. In fact, as early as 1973, those planning the move said that they would be requesting various services from the Government. Since the return ... the Settlement Committee has approached a number of Ministries [and departments] both directly and through [federal and provincial] riding representatives for the provision of services.
The expectations of receiving federal and provincial Government support for development of the community are quite high. I think this is reasonable to expect as the Governments have been significantly involved in community development in Fort Hope, Lansdowne House and Webequie for the past seven years. Residents of Summer Beaver expect the same response to their community as is directed at the other three communities.

However, the government's initial reaction to Summer Beaver was to take a 'wait-and-see' position, and for a short time it was questionable whether the people would get anything. We remember one DIAND official arguing that if government agencies supported the move, people in other villages might also move. The result would be a proliferation of new communities that the government would be forced to support, and he made it clear that he felt this would be 'an abrogation of our responsibility to the Canadian taxpayer.' He also said that the people of Summer Beaver should be encouraged to return to Lansdowne, regardless of the trouble that might ensue.

This view apparently was also held by senior DIAND officials, because it was over a year before any DIAND programs were offered in the village and, in the interim, pressure was put on other government agencies not to become involved. As a Manpower official told us: 'Meetings were held with us and other departments by DIAND to at least wait and see. They felt we should hold out for as long as we could. Their thinking was, if the people wanted to go and set up a community, then we should have as little to do with them as possible.'

Luckily for the people of Summer Beaver, the hard-line policy was not adopted by other government departments. Realizing that it would be in the best interests of everyone concerned to give the community support, Manpower and finally DIAND did begin to provide their services. Since then, other agencies have followed suit. In fact, by the time the community was two years old it had almost everything the government had to give. There was a nursing station, a school, postal service, a portable sawmill, government jobs, a housing program, social assistance, and even make-work and community-development programs. It was as if the last fifteen years in the band's history had been compressed into two. The price that the people of Summer Beaver were willing to pay to live on their own was high, but nothing they could escape. When it came to their economic survival, they knew that the government had to be involved.

A sick community

Meanwhile, back in Lansdowne, things had gone from bad to worse. For instance, in 1976 there was an incredibly high number of criminal and liquor charges in the community – 52 and 21 respectively – whereas in Summer Beaver there were none. And this was in spite of the fact that the exodus to Summer Beaver had reduced the population of Lansdowne to about 200.

At one point in 1976 there were eight people from Lansdowne in jail. A closer look at the eight and what they were serving time for gives at least some indication of how difficult life in the community had become: a seventeen-year-old boy was serving six months for breaking and entering; a twenty-one-year-old woman was serving eighteen months for the same crime; three young men, two eighteen and one nineteen, were serving six months for providing alcohol to minors (one of them was also charged with sexual assault); a twenty-one-year-old man was serving eighteen months for breaking into the Hudson's Bay store and attacking three nuns who had come to Lansdowne to do social work; another man, twenty-six, was serving eighteen months for attempting to murder his wife (once in Lansdowne he tried to choke her; another time he attacked her in the south, and when the two were back in Lansdowne, he chased her with an axe while he was drunk); finally, still another man, twenty-four, was serving eighteen months for attempting to murder his brother and then trying to commit suicide by shooting himself in the stomach. Even when the police reacted by increasing their patrols and threatening to make more arrests, the situation still did not improve.

A plea for help

By the summer of 1976 the community was in desperate shape, and as a last resort, the older Catholics, now ready to try anything, wrote to the prime minister for help:

Dear Prime Minister Trudeau:
We are all writing to you from Lansdowne House about how things are going. We have been trying to discuss our problems in our settlement and would ask to have Lansdowne made into a reserve because there is always trouble here.
  The reason why there is always trouble has to do with the liquor. We concluded that different places are needed for people who don't drink. That's the way we see it. Some people disturb the old people when they drink. We think it's better to make another place for these people. When there are new houses built here there are always windows broken.
  We would like to ask you something. Is there a way to stop the liquor for the Indian? We want to know about it. Especially since there are no resident OPP up here. Also, when people make money for their families a lot spend their money on liquor. And any person that is always drinking can't raise his family too well. We would like somebody to come up here and tell us how to improve things.
  This is the first time we, the Indian people of Lansdowne, have written to you. Would you answer as soon as possible, as soon as you get this letter?

Two months after they sent this pitiful letter, the people received the following terse reply from one of Mr Trudeau's secretaries:

Dear ...
On behalf of the Prime Minister, I wish to acknowledge your letter of July 26

concerning the problems you have encountered at Lansdowne House due to the misuse of alcohol by some people.

I am taking the liberty of forwarding copies of your letter to the Offices of the Minister of Indian and Northern Affairs and the Secretary of State for further consideration.

Thank you for writing to Mr Trudeau.

A more detailed letter, written by an administrative assistant to the minister of Indian Affairs, took two more months to arrive. In this letter it was pointed out that since Lansdowne was not a reserve, there was no legal way to prevent the residents from drinking. It was also pointed out that even if the community were a reserve, it would not necessarily follow that drinking would stop anyway. The letter went on to suggest that there were two programs that might work even if Lansdowne did not become a reserve: alcohol counselling, which already was in progress at the time, and Indian policing, a program in which an Indian police officer trained by the OPP would be stationed in the community at the government's expense.

One month later the residents were paid a follow-up visit by a DIAND official who was sent there to discuss possible solutions to the problems in Lansdowne. But as it turned out, nothing new was added, either by the official or by the people. The consensus was that the community would have to continue with alcohol counselling, renew its request for a full-time Indian police officer, and continue to ask the federal government for reserve status. Yet over a year after this conversation, alcohol counselling had produced no tangible results, no Indian police officer had been assigned, and there was no change in the community's status. Lansdowne House was being ignored.

Death knell

By the end of 1977 the situation in Lansdowne had reached an all-time low. When trouble erupted, people left for the bush and stayed until it was safe to return. Finally, in November 1977, the community suffered yet another set-back when DIAND closed the school because of an attack on the white teachers by some of the trouble-makers. Lansdowne was now a newspaper headline in the south – 'VIOLENCE FORCES SCHOOL TO CLOSE.'

Taken together, these events convinced the government that Lansdowne was beyond repair, and its agencies began to withdraw their economic support. During the first few months of 1978 DIAND cancelled its economic-development programs and told the people that no new ones would be offered unless problems were solved. The Department of Manpower adopted a similar position and cancelled its BTSD courses for 1978. It also indicated that its make-work, job-training, and community-development programs would be harder to get. Even funding for the community's administrative officers and staff was reduced. The government was retrenching, and in doing so it was destroying the foundation of the community's carefully constructed artificial economy. A DIAND official who was working with the people at the time put it this way: 'Lansdowne House is a dying community and there's nothing anybody can do about it. Under the circumstances, the best thing the government can do is to expedite the process. These people will be far better off in other villages, or even in the south. I think it's up to the government to take things into its own hands. I don't think we can allow them to continue.'

All roads lead to government

The histories of Lansdowne House and Summer Beaver demonstrate the very real power that government officials have over the two villages and, by extension, over the rest of the band. True enough, it is likely that no matter what the government did, the breakaway of Summer Beaver from Lansdowne was inevitable, as was the violence in Lansdowne throughout the 1970s. But the histories of the two communities also show that the government alone can decide whether a community will get make-work, job-training, and community-development programs, and that the government alone, in the process, determines whether the community will survive. The histories of the two communities also show that the tie between government and the band is complete. Time and again we heard band leaders tell us that government power was absolute. In Lansdowne and Summer Beaver we found out just how true this is.

One final point: Recently a young man from Lansdowne became the settlement chairman, and under his leadership drinking and violence have been curtailed. He also began to negotiate with government to start up its programs, and although he has been fairly successful, it is still not clear whether the community will survive. In 1981 there were reports of new trouble, and today the feeling among government officials is still that Lansdowne is a bad risk – unpredictable, dangerous, and a community that may yet disappear.

8

Reflections

Fort Hope, Webequie, Lansdowne House, and Summer Beaver are remote and isolated places, with high unemployment, high welfare costs, and a low standard of living. They are places few people know about and even fewer visit. They are places where people wait for small planes to bring in the 'shuniah-ogama' – the money boss. They are places where people have lost control over their lives and where no one knows what will happen, except perhaps that without government support their communities will collapse. And yet they are places where people stay, not out of blind loyalty but because of what being members of a community means, for better or for worse. It is truly unfortunate and a monumental waste of human resources that they have been placed in a position in which they cannot be involved in the decisions that shape their lives.

We remember hearing a band official tell us about an upcoming meeting and how important it was, and then watching in silent awe as a government man stepped off a chartered plane alone, briefcase in hand, and within ten minutes was at a meeting in a cramped office where he became an autocrat and dictated what was going to happen. It was difficult to believe that government officials called this a consultation, especially the ones from the south who did not understand what life in the villages was like although their programs ultimately could determine whether or not a community would continue to exist. True enough, when we talked to these people, we got the impression that they felt they were doing the best they could, but what did this do to the people they were supposed to be serving?

If what we were told was correct, and what we saw true, the government's attitude towards the people generated a resigned acceptance on everyone's part that depending on government was a fact of life. It is perhaps a sad statement that never once in all the time we spent among the people did we hear of any plans to demonstrate against the government. But then, from their standpoint, dependency was not a theoretical issue; it was real. Certainly the people were unhappy with the power that government wielded and the tactics it used, but they were also quite frankly unwilling to complain too openly because of their fear of losing an important program.

What makes this even more disturbing is that ever since the White Paper was brought forward, the government has been much more concerned with implementation than planning. Almost everything has been ad hoc, and once again one must ask what impact this has had on the people. From what we saw, it made any attempt to improve economic conditions virtually useless. For example, whether or not a job-creation program was going to be offered was usually a last-minute decision taken by senior officials in Toronto or Ottawa, and this left the people wondering whether they were going to have money and work. Yet, since the band usually received some money for job-creation each year, there was enough of an incentive for the people to stay at home, uncertain and worried.

However, it need not be this way. The band villages are not without economic potential. Trapping, commercial fishing, and tourism are all endeavours with which band members are familiar and which can generate profits if managed properly. In the long term the economic potential is even greater. To the south of Fort Hope, below the Albany River, Kimberly-Clark is harvesting large amounts of timber for use in its mills. The company likely will be cutting near the reserve within the next five years, and the band is considering building a road to join one that the company is building. Another company, Keezic Resources, is currently investigating a gold deposit in the reserve. Both developments could translate into revitalized communities where jobs and opportunities to start new businesses are not just dreams.

But all this depends on the government. Will DIAND, Manpower, and other government agencies help the people plan for these developments and others yet to come? Will they provide the people with adequate resources to take advantage of these opportunities? Will they develop clear and workable objectives? Will they monitor their programs? Will they promote local control? Will they consult with the people? Or will they continue to offer inflexible programs that work at cross purposes and against any real chance for economic independence and success?

Notes

Preface

1 Hawthorn *A Survey of the Contemporary Indians of Canada* vol 1, 45
2 Ibid vol 2, 21
3 Ibid vol 1, 14
4 The title of the White Paper is *Statement of the Government of Canada on Indian Policy*. For a thorough account of the genesis of the White Paper see Weaver *Making Canadian Indian Policy*.
5 Canada Employment and Immigration Commission *The Development of an Employment Policy for Indian, Inuit and Métis People* 12
6 National Indian Brotherhood *Submission to the Parliamentary Task Force on Employment Opportunities for the '80s* 6
7 Cardinal *The Rebirth of Canada's Indians* 55
8 A band of Indians is a legally constituted group '(a) for whose use and benefit in common, lands, the legal title to which is vested in Her Majesty [the Queen], have been set apart, on or after the 4th day of September 1951, (b) for whose use and benefit in common, moneys are held by Her Majesty, or (c) declared by the Governor in Council to be a band for the purposes of ... [the Indian Act].' Canada *The Indian Act* 1
9 The Department of Manpower and Immigration is now called Canada Employment and Immigration Commission.

Chapter 1

1 Canada DIAND *Registered Indian Population by Sex and Residence* xvii
2 Although 1,965 people belong to the band, 628 members live elsewhere than in the band communities. Ibid 00024

3 'Reserve means a tract of land, the legal title to which is vested in Her Majesty [the Queen] that has been set apart for the use and benefit of a band.' Canada *The Indian Act* 2

4 Although all of the band communities are located on Crown land, only the Fort Hope Reserve is located on federal crown land. The others are located on Ontario Crown land, which means that the government of Ontario rather than the government of Canada has jurisdiction over the area. For a thorough discussion of this issue see Ollivier *British North America Acts and Selected Statutes 1867-1962* 88ff. Despite the jurisdictional difference, the band villages generally receive the same government services.

5 Canada DIAND *Nakina District*

6 Ontario Ministry of Natural Resources *West Patricia Land Use Plan* 13

7 Ibid

8 Ibid

9 Ibid

10 The police justify tying people up on the grounds that there is no jail in the community and no other way to hold prisoners without them being able to escape.

11 *The Chronicle-Journal* (Thunder Bay) 28 October 1977, 1

12 Boyer 'Canada's Keystone: Ontario' 787

Chapter 2

1 The aboriginal Ojibwa were composed of several groups of people who lived along both the north and south shores of Lake Superior. Since the members of the Fort Hope Band are descendants of the people on the north shore, we will limit our attention to their aboriginal life-style in this chapter. Usually scholars refer to the Indians on the north shore as Northern Ojibwa and those on the south shore as Chippewa.

2 Bishop *The Northern Ojibwa and the Fur Trade* 7

3 Ibid

4 Hickerson *The Chippewa and their Neighbours* 40

5 Rogers 'Ojibwa Culture' 35

6 According to one group of scholars, rules for the ownership of land did not appear among tribes such as the Ojibwa until they became involved in the fur trade. See, for example, Bishop 'The Emergence of Hunting Territories among the Northern Ojibwa,' Hickerson 'Land Tenure of the Rainy Lake Chippewa at the Beginning of the 19th Century,' Leacock *The Montagnais 'Hunting Territory' and the Fur Trade*, and Rogers *The Hunting Group–Hunting Territory Complex among the Mistassini Indians*. Although no longer widely supported, another group of scholars has argued that land ownership existed in pre-contact times as well. See, for

example, Cooper 'Is the Algonkian Family Hunting Ground System Pre-Colum-
bian?' Hallowell 'The Size of Algonkian Hunting Territories,' Speck 'The Family
Hunting Band as the Basis of Algonkian Social Organization,' and Speck and
Eiseley 'The Significance of the Hunting Territory System of the Algonkians in
Social Theory.'

7 Technically, 'for a group to constitute a genuine clan it must conform to three
major specifications. If any one of the three is lacking, the group is not a clan,
however greatly it may resemble one in composition and external appearance.
In the first place, it must be based explicitly on a unilineal rule of descent which
unites its central core of members ... In the second place, to constitute a clan a
group must have residential unity ... In the third place, the group must exhibit
actual social integration. It cannot be a mere unorganized aggregation of independent families like those residing in ... [a] residential suburb. There must be positive
group sentiment [objectively expressed in regular and recurrent interaction], and
in particular the in-marrying spouses must be recognized as an integral part of the
membership.' Murdock *Social Structure* 68

8 Levi-Strauss *Totemism* 19

9 See Rogers 'Leadership among the Indians of Eastern Subarctic Canada.'

10 Rogers 'Ojibwa Culture' 35

11 See Hlady *Indian Migrations in Manitoba and the West.*

12 Although the Objiwa were moving into a region that already had been exploited by
the Cree, it still contained valuable furs. 'Because of their long specialization as
intermediaries in the fur trade, many of the Cree were not particularly skillful as
trappers, and in fact had developed a disdain for this activity. Not surprisingly,
therefore, when the growing size of the fur-trade network generated a large demand
for provisions, many of the [Cree] bands which formerly had exploited the bison
resource of the [western] parklands only on a seasonal basis moved into the latter
region where they could serve as provisioners for the trading companies. The
Ojibwa, on the other hand, were more proficient fur hunters, and the trading companies, especially the North West Company, actively encouraged them to move
into Cree territory. Many Ojibwa did so, and with their more intensive trapping
they were able to secure furs in hunting grounds which the Cree had reported to be
exhausted. This combination of circumstances possibly explains not only why the
Ojibwa bands moved from one impoverished department to another, which was
presumably equally depleted, but it could also account for the peaceful nature of
these incursions. With their different economic orientations, the two groups would
not have come into serious conflict.' Ray *Indians in the Fur Trade* 102–4

13 Ibid

14 Scholars continue to disagree about the boundaries of aboriginal Ojibwa territory.
The position we have adopted is based on information contained in Bishop *The*

Northern Ojibwa and the Fur Trade, and Hickerson *The Chippewa and Their Neighbours*. It also has been suggested that the aboriginal Ojibwa occupied territory north of the height of land prior to their involvement in the fur trade. For more information regarding the latter interpretation see Dawson 'An Application of the Direct Historical Approach to the Algonkians of Northern Ontario.'

15 Rogers 'Leadership among the Indians of Eastern Subarctic Canada' 274–5
16 Since neither the North West Company nor the Hudson's Bay Company was able to impose strict limits on the price they paid for furs at each of their posts, competition took place both between and within the companies. Under these circumstances Ojibwa trapping units were far more mobile than they might have been if competition had existed only between the companies. See Ray *Indians in the Fur Trade* 61–70.
17 The disappearance of the game was likely due to a combination of factors, including forest fires, over-hunting, and disease among the animals. See Bishop *The Northern Ojibwa and the Fur Trade* 277–84.
18 See Rogers and Black 'Subsistence Strategy in the Fish and Hare Period.'
19 Bishop *The Northern Ojibwa and the Fur Trade* 284
20 North West Company posts were established at the present location of Fort Hope and Webequie between 1800 and 1820. When the North West and Hudson's Bay companies merged in 1821, the posts came under the jurisdiction of the Bay. See Voorhis *Historical Forts and Trading Companies* 82ff.
21 Skinner *Notes on the Eastern Cree and Northern Saulteaux* 150
22 See Long *Treaty No. 9.*
23 Holding Indian status refers to being registered as an Indian or entitled to be registered as an Indian. Registration is based on both patrilineal and affinal considerations, patrilineal in so far as anyone who is a descendant of a registered Indian father is entitled to be registered, and any woman who marries a registered Indian man also is entitled to be registered. In fact, when a registered Indian woman marries a non-Indian, she is enfranchised automatically – that is, she is removed from the list of registered Indians kept by DIAND and paid a per capita share of the funds that are held in trust for her band. Canada *The Indian Act* 2–10. Enfranchised Indians lose their Indian rights, including 'the right to live on the reserve, ... to receive moneys, ... have free medical care, free education, ... [and be exempt] from income tax for all funds earned on the reserve, and from property tax on the reserve.' Nagler *Natives without a Home* 6
24 Canada *The James Bay Treaty* 7
25 Ibid

Chapter 3

1 Canada *The James Bay Treaty* 21
2 The Ontario Ministry of Natural Resources keeps records of the band's fur and animal harvests. Figure 1 is based on these records.
3 Interfering with the mail is against the law. It was possible only because post offices in the band villages were located in Hudson's Bay buildings.
4 Although the annuity is distributed by the federal government, the money is provided by Ontario.
5 Aside from the annuity, the cash value of these benefits has increased in recent years. For more information see Brown *A Chronology of Social Welfare and Related Legislation*, and Canada DIAND *Consolidation of Legislation Pertaining to Native Peoples*.
6 Canada *Statement of the Government of Canada on Indian Policy* 5
7 Ibid 6
8 Ibid
9 Indian Chiefs of Alberta *Citizens Plus*
10 Union of British Columbia Indian Chiefs *A Declaration of Indian Rights*
11 Winnipeg 1971
12 See Cardinal *The Unjust Society*.
13 House of Commons *Debates* 28th Parliament, 2nd session, vol 2, 1412
14 United States *House Concurrent Resolution 108*
15 See, for example, Forbes *The Indian in America's Past* 112–41, and Wax and Buchanan *Solving 'The Indian Problem'* 67–92.
16 Quoted in Forbes *The Indian in America's Past* 128.
17 Ibid 121
18 Quoted in Wax and Buchanan *Solving 'The Indian Problem'* 87–8.
19 These figures are based on information contained in Canada Department of Industry, Trade, and Commerce *1970–1971 Canada Year Book* and *Canada Year Book 1978–1979*.
20 Canada DIAND *Indian Conditions* 56ff
21 National Indian Brotherhood *Submission to the Parliamentary Task Force on Employment Opportunities for the '80s* 8
22 Ibid
23 'The Unfinished Tapestry – Indian Policy in Canada' speech by the Honourable Jean Chrétien, minister of Indian Affairs and Northern Development, presented at Queen's University, Kingston, Ontario, 17 March 1971, 10–11

Chapter 4

1 There are only slight differences in the amount of money that comes into the band villages from make-work, job-training, and community-development programs as a proportion of total community income. In 1975, the proportions were all roughly 30 per cent.
2 The jobs were as follows: 1 chief, 1 band manager, 2 settlement chairmen, 5 councillors, 1 economic-development officer, 1 social-development officer, 1 constable, 2 secretaries, 3 employment advisers, 4 community-health workers, 2 nurse's aides, 3 teacher's aides, 1 handyman, 1 housemaid, and 9 janitors.
3 Since the money that is allocated via welfare and social-assistance programs is fixed by federal and provincial legislation, band administrators spend most of their administrative effort trying to increase the flow of make-work, job-training, and community-development programs into the band.
4 'Contrary to popular beliefs, the main source of funding for employment programs available to status Indians is already with Canada Employment and Immigration Commission ... DIAND budgeted $7.5 million for training, placement and mobility in 1975–76 ... [whereas] the Department of Manpower and Immigration spent $9.0 million on training for status Indians in 1974–75 and $12.2 million in 1975–76.' Canada Employment and Immigration Commission *The Development of an Employment Policy for Indian, Inuit and Métis People* 11
5 National Indian Socio-Economic Development Committee *To Have What Is One's Own* 22–3

Chapter 5

1 Our evaluation of the businesses is based on business records, DIAND reports, and verbal statements made by key participants.
2 In order to protect the anonymity of our sources, we will not provide specific references for internal government reports.
3 The Indian Community Secretariat is now called the Native Community Branch. It is part of the Ontario Ministry of Citizenship and Culture.
4 Like other White Paper initiatives, this one also can be traced to the United States. In fact, the Canadian proposal bears a striking resemblance to the contents of a report that was submitted to the Kennedy administration in 1961. The report, titled *Report to the Secretary of the Interior by the Task Force on Indian Affairs, July 10, 1961*, was commissioned by Secretary of the Interior Udall as a result of campaign promises made by President Kennedy. On 12 July 1961, Secretary Udall summed up the contents of the report: 'Calling attention to the serious shortage of employment opportunities for Indians, the report recommends development of

Indian-owned resources, more vigorous efforts to attract industries to reservation areas, and an expanded program of vocational training and placement. It also calls for the creation of a Special Reservation Development Loan Fund maintained by the Bureau of Indian Affairs.' Quoted in Forbes *The Indian in America's Past* 129.

5 This problem arises because of the Indians' unique constitutional relationship with the government of Canada. According to our constitution, the Parliament of Canada has almost unlimited authority when it comes to regulating Indian land. One observer puts it this way: 'It may be generally stated that so long as there is a predominant Indian presence or interest in reserve land, the Parliament of Canada is completely free to enact whatever system, or even systems, of land tenure it deems to be most appropriate. In other words, there is no constitutional limitation of Parliament's authority in this field.' Henderson *Land Tenure in Indian Reserves* 6. Given this broad authority, Parliament has chosen to implement a system of tenure on reserves which prevents Indians from selling land on an individual basis and only allows an Indian band to dispose of its land with federal approval. This makes it virtually impossible for Indians to pledge their land as collateral. Moreover, for Indians on provincial Crown land the problem is even more complicated because they do not have any ownership rights to the land they occupy. Nor do they control the resources they use, since the authority to regulate resources on provincial Crown land is constitutionally vested in the provinces.

6 Canada *Statement of the Government of Canada on Indian Policy* 10

7 Ibid

8 Canada DIAND *Indian Conditions* 71

9 Hickling-Johnson *Review of Sectoral Programs and Economic Development Corporations* 5

10 Canada *Report of the Auditor General of Canada to the House of Commons* 171

11 Hickling-Johnson *Review of Sectoral Programs and Economic Development Corporations* 5

12 Under the regulations governing the ICS, it could not act as a primary adviser to the co-op.

13 The person DIAND hired was a retired carpenter. He quit because the work he was required to do was more than he was prepared to undertake at that stage in his life.

14 DIAND rationalized this decision on the grounds that if it became involved in formal negotiations with the contractors, the opening of the supermarket would have to be delayed.

15 Although Fort Hope is a dry reserve, the three men allegedly smuggled liquor in by hiding it in their tool chests.

16 Grand Council Treaty 9 is an Indian organization that represents the people whose ancestors agreed to Treaty No 9.

17 Since commercial fishing off-reserve falls under the jurisdiction of the provincial

government, it was the Ministry of Natural Resources rather than a federal department that issued commercial fishing licences to the band.

18 This was done under the auspices of a Work Opportunities Program, which permits
'the use of social assistance funding to supplement wages in community projects
for those who would otherwise be supported by welfare.' Canada DIAND *Indian
Conditions* 29

Chapter 6

1 At times the committee was buttressed by one representative each from the federal
Department of Regional Economic Expansion and the provincial Ministry of Treasury, Economics, and Intergovernmental Affairs.
2 Pappert 'Ottawa's Great LEAP Backward'
3 Ibid 42
4 Axworthy 'Axworthy Leaps to LEAP's Defence'
5 Pappert 'Ann Pappert Replies'
6 The inn-restaurant and the Fort Hope camps were managed by five people, the
Webequie camps by two, the Ogoki camps by one, and the Lansdowne camps by
one.
7 *Evaluation for LEAP of the Fort Hope Development Corporation* Fort Hope Development Corporation files
8 Ibid

Chapter 7

1 The small encampments the people came from had traditionally been 'occupied for
ten or more months of the year. The only time they were vacated was during a
summer visit to Lansdowne House, which began just before the arrival of the Treaty
Party and lasted anywhere from a few weeks to a few months. During the winter
trapping season the men and older boys left the ... [encampments] for periods
which varied from two to ten days in order to visit their traplines. However, most
of the women and children remained behind in the settlements.' Taylor 'Northern
Ojibwa Communities of the Contact-Traditional Period' 22
2 This is a pseudonym.
3 In fact, the Anglicans were involved in a revitalization movement. Such movements
have been reported in primitive and modern societies throughout the course of
history and 'are deliberate organized attempts by some members of a society to
construct a more satisfying culture by rapid acceptance of a pattern of multiple
innovations.' Wallace *Culture and Personality* 143–4. For more information on
revitalization movements see Wallace 'Revitalization Movements.'
4 *The Chronicle-Journal* (Thunder Bay) 15 March 1978, 5

Bibliography

Axworthy, Lloyd 'Lloyd Axworthy leaps to LEAP's Defence: When a Co-op Is not a Co-op' *Canadian Business* 54 no 1 (1981) 9–10

Bishop, Charles A. 'The Emergence of Hunting Territories among the Northern Ojibwa' *Ethnology* 9 (1970) 1–15

– *The Northern Ojibwa and the Fur Trade: An Historical and Ecological Study.* Toronto: Holt, Rinehart and Winston 1974

Boyer, David S. 'Canada's Keystone: Ontario' *National Geographic* 154 no 6 (1978) 760–95

Brown, Ruth *A Chronology of Social Welfare and Related Legislation, 1908–1974: Selected Federal Statutes.* Ottawa: Health and Welfare Canada, Policy and Program Development and Co-ordination Branch 1975

Canada *The James Bay Treaty, Treaty No. 9 (Made in 1905 and 1906), and Adhesions Made in 1929 and 1930.* Ottawa: Queen's Printer 1964

– *Statement of the Government of Canada on Indian Policy 1969.* Ottawa: Queen's Printer 1969

– *The Indian Act* rev to 1970. Ottawa: Queen's Printer 1970

– *Report of the Auditor General of Canada to the House of Commons.* Ottawa: Queen's Printer 1980

Canada Department of Indian Affairs and Northern Development *Nakina District.* Geraldton, Ont: Nakina District Office 1976

– *Consolidation of Legislation Pertaining to Native Peoples.* Ottawa: Office of Native Claims 1978

– *Indian Conditions: A Survey.* Ottawa 1980

– *Registered Indian Population by Sex and Residence.* Ottawa: Reserves and Trusts, Indian and Inuit Affairs Program 1981

Canada Department of Industry, Trade, and Commerce *1970–1971 Canada Year Book.* Ottawa 1971

– *Canada Year Book 1978–1979*. Ottawa 1978
Canada Employment and Immigration Commission *The Development of an Employment Policy for Indian, Inuit and Métis People*. Ottawa 1978
Cardinal, Harold *The Unjust Society: The Tragedy of Canada's Indians*. Edmonton: Hurtig 1969
– *The Rebirth of Canada's Indians*. Edmonton: Hurtig 1977
Cooper, John M. 'Is the Algonkian Family Hunting Ground System Pre-Columbian?' *American Anthropologist* 41 (1939) 66–90
Dawson, K.C.A. 'An Application of the Direct Historical Approach to the Algonkians of Northern Ontario' *Canadian Journal of Archaeology* 1 (1977) 151–81
Forbes, Jack D. (ed) *The Indian in America's Past*. Englewood Cliffs, NJ: Prentice-Hall 1964
Hallowell, A. Irving 'The Size of Algonkian Hunting Territories: A Function of Ecological Adjustment' *American Anthropologist* 51 (1949) 35–45
Hawthorn, H.B. (ed) *A Survey of the Contemporary Indians of Canada: A Report on Economic, Political and Educational Needs and Policies* 2 vols. Ottawa: Queen's Printer 1966–67
Henderson, William H. *Land Tenure in Indian Reserves*. Ottawa: DIAND Research Branch, Policy and Evaluation Group 1978
Hickerson, Harold 'Land Tenure of the Rainy Lake Chippewa at the Beginning of the 19th Century' *Smithsonian Contributions to Anthropology* 2 (1967) 37–63
– *The Chippewa and Their Neighbours: A Study in Ethnohistory*. New York: Holt, Rinehart and Winston 1970
Hickling-Johnson Management Consultants *A Review of Sectoral Programs and Economic Development Corporations*. Toronto 1978
Hlady, Walter M. *Indian Migrations in Manitoba and the West*. Historical and Scientific Society of Manitoba, series 3, nos 17 and 18, Winnipeg 1964
Indian Chiefs of Alberta *Citizens Plus*. Edmonton: Alberta Indian Association 1970
Leacock, Eleanor *The Montagnais 'Hunting Territory' and the Fur Trade*. American Anthropological Association, memoir 78, Washington 1964
Levi-Strauss, Claude *Totemism*. Boston: Beacon Press 1962
Long, John *Treaty No. 9: The Indian Petitions*. Cobalt, Ont: Highway Book Shop 1978
Manitoba Indian Brotherhood *Wahbung: Our Tomorrows*. Winnipeg 1971
Murdock, George P. *Social Structure*. New York: Macmillan 1949
Nagler, Mark *Natives without a Home*. Don Mills, Ont: Longmans 1975
National Indian Brotherhood *Submission to the Parliamentary Task Force on Employment Opportunities for the '80s*. Ottawa, 13 February 1981
National Indian Socio-Economic Development Committee *To Have What Is One's Own*. Ottawa 1979

Ollivier, M. *British North America Acts and Selected Statutes 1867–1962*. Ottawa: Queen's Printer 1962

Ontario Ministry of Natural Resources *West Patricia Land Use Plan: Background Papers*. Toronto 1981

Pappert, Ann 'Ottawa's Great LEAP Backward' *Canadian Business* 53 no 11 (1980) 42ff

– 'Ann Pappert Replies' *Canadian Business* 54 no 1 (1981) 10–11

Ray, Arthur J. *Indians in the Fur Trade: Their Role as Trappers, Hunters and Middlemen in the Lands Southwest of Hudson Bay, 1660–1870*. Toronto: University of Toronto Press 1974

Rogers, Edward S. *The Hunting Group–Hunting Territory Complex among the Mistassini Indians*. National Museum of Canada, Bulletin 195, Anthropological Series, Ottawa 1963

– 'Leadership among the Indians of Eastern Subarctic Canada' *Anthropologica* 7 (1965) 263–84

– 'Ojibwa Culture: The Traditional Culture History' in *Kenora 1967, Resolving Conflicts – A Cross-Cultural Approach*. Winnipeg: University of Manitoba, Department of University Extension and Adult Education 1967

Rogers, Edward S. and Mary J. Black 'Subsistence Strategy in the Fish and Hare Period, Northern Ontario; The Weagamow Ojibwa, 1880–1920' *Journal of Anthropological Research* 1 (1976) 1–43

Skinner, Alanson *Notes on the Eastern Cree and Northern Saulteaux*. Anthropological Papers of the American Museum of Natural History, vol 9 part 1, New York 1911

Speck, Frank 'The Family Hunting Band as the Basis of Algonkian Social Organization' *American Anthropologist* 17 (1915) 289–305

Speck, Frank and Loren C. Eisely 'The Significance of the Hunting Territory System of the Algonkians in Social Theory' *American Anthropologist* 41 (1939) 557–600

Taylor, J. Garth 'Northern Ojibwa Communities of the Contact-Traditional Period' *Anthropologica* 14 (1972) 19–30

Union of British Columbia Indian Chiefs *A Declaration of Indian Rights: The B.C. Indian Position Paper*. Victoria 1970

United States *House Concurrent Resolution 108*. Washington: United States Government Printing Office 1953

Voorhis, Ernest *Historical Forts and Trading Companies*. Ottawa: Department of the Interior, National Resources Intelligence Branch 1930

Wallace, Anthony F.C. *Culture and Personality*. New York: Random House 1961

– 'Revitalization Movements' *American Anthropologist* 66 (1964) 264–81

Wax, Murray and Robert W. Buchanan *Solving 'The Indian Problem': The White Man's Burdensome Business*. New York: New York Times Company 1975

Weaver, Sally M. *Making Canadian Indian Policy: The Hidden Agenda 1968–70*. Toronto: University of Toronto Press 1981

Index